Craftswomen in Kerdassa, Egypt

Women, Work and Development, 7

Craftswomen in Kerdassa, Egypt

Household production and reproduction

Patricia D. Lynch with Hoda Fahmy

Undertaken under the auspices of the
Center for Egyptian Civilisation Studies
and with the financial support of the
United Nations Fund for Population Activities
(UNFPA)

International Labour Office   Geneva

ISBN 92-2-103625-1
ISSN 0253-2042

First published 1984

Printed in Switzerland

PREFACE

This study forms one of a series on women's roles and demographic issues emanating from a global research project supported by the United Nations Fund for Population Activities. It was undertaken under the auspices of the Center for Egyptian Civilization Studies. Nawal M. Hassan served as Project Director. The contributions of women in an Egyptian community to subsistence activities and handicraft production are described, as are changes in labour processes which increasingly push women into less rewarding forms of work. The demographic implications of these conditions are assessed.

The authors provide ethnographic evidence on a set of Moslem women craft workers in an Egyptian village, regarding women's work and how it relates to childbearing and rearing activities. They contend that the kind of information they provide at the individual and household levels is important for providing policy-relevant insights into existing impediments to expansion of household production or the involvement of women in the paid labour force, as well as vocational, health and family planning programmes.

A significant finding of this micro-study is the positive correlation between women's involvement in household production and pregnancy, spontaneous abortion and infant death. One explanation given by the women themselves for bearing children is that they feel the need for additional child labour to increase their productivity. Those involved in subsistence craft work, lacking long-term economic security, are unable to plan their lives with regard to childbirth as well as material survival. Again, the authors point to the domination of husbands in family planning matters when they are also dominant financially.

Access to income-generating work is seen as a key to enabling lower status women to gain security and decision-making capacity. Better basic health care is also viewed as essential for lowering infant death rates and female mortality, which are inextricably linked to family planning motivation. Relevant education and vocational training programmes and co-operative formation are stressed as essential components for improving the economic and demographic situation of any overall policy.

The authors underline the need for further investigation of the nature of relations within the domestic group, to increase understanding of domestic power processes in rural areas and to show how these are linked to divisions of labour, resource allocation, fertility levels and family planning acceptance.

Acknowledgement

We wish to thank the Population and Labour Policies Branch of the Employment and Development Department of the International Labour Office for supporting this work and the Center for Egyptian Civilization Studies for sponsoring it. Particular thanks are due to Nawal Hassan who had close contact with the project from conception to completion and without whose advice and assistance the project could not have been completed, and to Christine Oppong for her work in co-ordinating the collation and presentation of data.

Patricia D. Lynch
Hoda Fahmy

CONTENTS

I. INTRODUCTION

Egypt has one of the longest histories of petty commodity production in the world and yet there is not much known of the role which women's labour has played in these productive processes. Because of the long literary history and the particular nature of record keeping, many aspects of production are well documented, especially in comparison with other areas of the world. Yet, even recent attempts to direct theories of social scientists to Egypt's past and present have failed to address the question of women's participation in production. A major stumbling block has been acceptance by women as well as men of definitions of work which omit, from statistics compiled, productive activities within the domestic domain, as well as much of women's unpaid family labour in trading and agriculture. Thus an impression is given that women's contribution to production and "development" is mainly confined to "housework", subsistence and child-rearing.

Work, its definition, recording and measurement in different cultural contexts, is now an important focus of concern in several disciplines, including in particular the non-wage and household activities of women. Anthropologists have been among those social scientists who have been guilty of representing only one-half of the world's population. They now share a widespread concern both to improve the conceptualisation and documentation of work[1] and production processes and to give due regard to women as well as men, which should facilitate full understanding of the nature of culture and society or the relationship between "traditional" society and present processes of change.

Tucker (1976) has mentioned that Egyptian women in the past were known to take over small craft businesses on the death of their husbands, and had a significant role to play in textile production, Egypt's most widespread domestic industry. Staffa's (1977) important historical analysis on Cairo devotes considerable space to understanding the relationship between forces of production, distribution, and consumption in craft production, and some attention to the further relation between these and the state, yet she ignores the consequences of organisation upon the basic unit of production, the domestic unit. Baer (1964) has produced a definitive work on craft organisation in Ottoman Egypt with no consideration for the role of women.

Interest in cross-cultural women's studies has lately increased because of western concern with women's status. A strikingly low participation by women in the Middle East workforce generally has been noted, although there is a great degree of fluctuation from country to country in official statistics. It is sometimes believed that the participation of women in paid labour will facilitate healthy development and lower birth rates, which are major problems in these areas (Beck and Keddie, 1978; Youssef, 1974). Others question these assumptions on the grounds that *sources* are very inconsistent and sometimes conflicting (Buvinic, 1976). There is also disagreement on the relationship between social values and women's participation. Two of the most prominent anthropologists, in recent work, take opposite sides on this question. Youssef (1974) finds the participation of women in paid non-agricultural labour related to neither economic development nor to the wife-mother role in the

1

Middle East (that is, to marital and fertility characteristics), but to differences in social structure and ideology. Youssef says, "Female employment rates were low because all women were restricted, regardless of age, marital condition, or motherhood status". Peters (Beck and Keddie, 1978), on the other hand, believes that the social structure is equally constricting for both sexes at certain periods in the life cycle or in the domestic cycle, and that economic diversity is the determining factor in differences among the four areas of the Middle East which he studied.

Beck and Keddie (1978) note several important general conclusions based on ethnographic evidence of women in the Middle East. The position of women who consume and do not produce, and the general attitude towards them as childbearing instruments, affect the living standards of the entire economy. They believe that law reform and female education correlate with women's paid employment and lowered birth rates. Women's participation has not kept pace with that of men in the change to wage labour that has occurred during industrialisation, and this is a serious problem for women. In this area, studies of indigenous organisation may suggest creative ways to share housekeeping and child-care duties and to seek good part-time jobs or plan new employment. Fuller female participation is also needed to lessen the gap which is increasing between incomes of upper and lower classes. In the Middle East husbands often decide if a wife can work for wages, at what kind of job, and if she can use her wages. Men have a legal as well as a religious right to do so (Beck and Keddie, 1978), a situation which makes women's status precarious. Beck and Keddie also believe that capitalism has had a different effect on women's labour than it has on men's and, for this reason must be studied separately.

Buvinic (1976) warns that women's status cannot be inferred from the degree of participation in economic activities alone. This is especially true if we go beyond her more narrow definition of participation which is defined in existing statistics. She calls for a more careful analysis of women's control over specific productive activities, the extent to which these activities are perceived indispensable to society, the possession by women of technical expertise necessary for different types of production, their relative control over the means of production and distribution, and the key variables of a non-economic nature which are related to women's participation.

Few of these issues have been addressed in Egypt, where only 4.8 per cent of the current modern workforce and 3.6 per cent of non-agricultural employment are female (White in Beck and Keddie, 1978). The workforce in small manufacturing establishments is mainly composed of adult males (Mabro and Radwan, 1976), that is, 86.4 per cent, as opposed to 6.1 per cent children under 15 years and 7.4 per cent adult females. Of this figure, 59 per cent are employed in rural areas. According to Mabro and Radwan, 59 per cent of all women who work are in dressmaking, 16 per cent are in spinning and weaving, and 8 per cent in other textile industries. No major cottage or household industry exists in rural areas, and the small manufacturing sector in Egypt does not, as in many other developing countries, "provide employment opportunities that lead to higher participation by the population in the labour force" (Mabro and Radwan, 1976). Few, if any, statistics exist in Egypt on the skill structure for either men or women.

Women's work in one delta village was determined by age, marital status and socio-economic status of kin group (Morsy in Beck and Keddie, 1978). The female economic contribution is considered supplementary and women do not act as a corporate group in any economic enterprise nor do they have any control over the

2

product of their labour. Because male labour is considered more vital, it can be assigned a monetary value, and often is, whereas women's work is not, even when it contributes to a product marketed by the husband (Morsy in Beck and Keddie, 1978).

In Egypt, "Female activities in the home or in agriculture still constitute a large part of the 'invisible' national income" (Tucker, 1976). Tucker fears an ever-widening gap between the public and private sectors with women gaining little opportunity to work outside the home. The female contribution to the exchange value of the husband's labour is obscured by the fact that the work is unpaid (Gran, 1977), and statistics do not include, or grossly underestimate, many female activities (Tucker, 1976). Further, the process of industrialisation has changed the sexual division of labour.

Education, training, and cultural values also inhibit participation of women in the workforce, especially in rural areas, where women, who travel alone to work outside, may be subject to gossip, thus endangering their chances in the marriage market. This no villagers are willing to do, as marriage has a much higher priority than work. Few women are educated or trained for skilled jobs, but where they are, they are allowed more mobility because of the status these jobs bring. Due to the limited opportunities for suitable work for lower income and unskilled, uneducated women, they crowd into these areas and thus the price of their labour falls.

In home industry production for local markets, skills and production were related to age and experience, not to sex. But capital industry production has brought a more rigid division which fails to recruit women for skilled or well-paid jobs. They remain marginal workers, a pool of surplus labour.

Female participation in paid labour is higher in areas where factory work is limited, but "as factory work replaces home industry in a given area more women enter the factory but overall participation rate falls ... as home industry contracts displaced female workers are not absorbed by new factory industry — the European pattern of utilising cheap female labour in the early stages of industrialisation is not currently prevalent in Egypt" (Tucker, 1976).

Nagi (1971) has also stressed the poor position of women in industrial work, with women over 35 being pushed out of the market faster. Nagi explains this is as a "necessary" stage of industrialisation where men have the responsibility for "modernisation" and women may rejoin the labour market at a later "stage" of development. Surplus male labour, migration to urban centres, and marriage all lower women's participation. In rural areas, as household size increases, the number of workers also increases, but in urban areas this situation is reversed. Over a period of time, women's crude economic activity fell more than did men's, partly due to the younger population structure. The number of girls under 15 years employed in industry, especially in family craft businesses, increased greatly between 1937 and 1960. Illiterate and unskilled women in middle age have suffered most severely from changes in the labour structure. As laws of supply and demand operate ineffectively in the rural labour market, workers are recruited from the "undifferentiated rural surplus". Government policies in 1971 were benefiting only an elite of industrial and urban workers (Nagi, 1971).

The problems of measurement of female labour force participation in Egypt are severe. Western-oriented in education and lifestyle, government bureaucrats attempt to deal with rural issues which they little understand because of class and cultural differences. Capital- and technologically-intensive industry is fostered by the

3

government and by outside assistance. Structural models for collecting and analysing labour force participation data have been adopted, based on complex western societies little resembling Egypt, and planning based on these simplistic and erroneous concepts of "work" has proved to be a failure. Present models for collecting labour data on women ignore the complexity of activities women actually undertake, class and status differences in education, training, and socio-economic conditions and how these interact with women's work, area differences in the recruitment and utilisation of female labour, which in Egypt are broad, and attitudes to work which may help to explain women's desire to participate. Much of women's work is hidden because of denial or lack of recognition. No reasonable estimate has to date been forthcoming for the possible present productive contribution of Egyptian women. Because the family is a private realm which is jealously protected and because the social structure limits women's interaction in the social realm, small, household production is not easy to quantify or even identify.

Industries which are very small often fall outside the present government structure, and as women in rural areas are primarily employed in this group as unpaid family workers they are not counted in official statistics. Census surveys cannot efficiently identify female workers when neither they nor their husbands consider that they are working, but rather consider they are only "helping out". This problem also masks female unemployment, as there is no way to identify how many rural women are seeking and unable to find income-generating activities. In fact, a recent estimate has put the figure for small and informal production at 60 per cent of the working population. As production by women is mostly ignored, this figure may be even higher.

Up to 95 per cent of rural women are illiterate, depending upon the area (Population Census, CAPMAS, 1976) and age, and vocational training for women is almost nonexistent. Training which does exist is mostly handled through the Ministry of Social Affairs, with 2,000 centres spread throughout Egypt. Despite good intentions, extremely limited funding and a higher focus on social welfare than expansion of production hampers the efficiency of this agency. Even occasional training programmes for women have little relevance to the real lives and values of rural women. For lower income, illiterate, and unskilled women there is literally no opportunity to work inside or outside the village, except in household or cottage industries in handicrafts or in petty trade, which occupy the highest number of women. To say, then, that Egypt has one of the lowest female participation rates in paid labour in the world does not really say much about what Egyptian women do.

Relationships between female involvement in work and fertility have also followed models derived from Western industrialised society where work means paid labour outside the home. Negative relationships between "work" and fertility are usually assumed, an oversight which we suggest is unwarranted from the evidence in the Egyptian case.

It is clear that there is a great lack of ethnographic evidence relating to the complex problems and issues presented. Working as economists normally do, from existing statistics, is bound to mislead us as to the amount of women's participation in work processes and in activities which contribute to market production. Cultural definitions of work need to be investigated more closely to see their relationship to economic change and their implicit assumptions regarding women. The variation of patterns of relationships within the household unit and effects of these patterns on

4

attitudes towards, and implementation of, family planning must be identified. Fertility statistics must be analysed in relation to type of work done and by socio-economic group, according to new and more meaningful categories of activity.

There is a great need for field studies which allow researchers access to households for long enough periods to observe women's activities throughout the yearly agricultural and production cycle. More information on local attitudes and values about work is essential. It is only through this means that data compilation may occur which will identify work patterns and their variations according to age, status group, household structure, and family and life cycle. Structural impediments to expansion of household production into small industry and to female involvement in paid labour may be identified and incorporated into more realistic labour policy, including an assessment and adjustment of present vocational training programmes for women. These issues affect not only the future lives of women, but the demographic structure and the quality of Egyptian life as a whole.

Approach to the problem

The study is qualitative and empirical. This means it depends upon anthropological methods of observation and recording under conditions of long-term contact to determine women's productive and reproductive roles and their attitudes and concepts regarding these roles. Key informants, observation and structured interviews were used to situate local cases in a wider economic context. A brief description of the case studies is presented in the appendix to demonstrate the complexity of social, economic and ideological factors which determine individual life choices. The study attempts to record the material conditions of life in specific conditions and at one historical moment in Egypt. The location was chosen as a focus of study because it was believed to be representative of certain conditions of development and change. We believe that developing links with the world market have effects upon social relations within the area under study and that the nature of social relations, in turn, affects the rate at which capitalisation takes place.

We have differentiated between women in the study according to indicators which exist within a culturally homogeneous area. This is difficult where women dress almost identically and where modes of behaviour, consumption, and lifestyle are highly institutionalised. We have chosen groupings which we term "classes" or "status groups" according to education, income (where this could be accurately assessed), and property (land, buildings, animals, household furnishings, size and condition, gold jewellery, clothing). We found, however, that there were differences in some cases between our assessment and that of village assistants, and this has been noted. We suggest here that purely material indicators are inadequate to describe the social differentiation as defined in village terms. For this reason we added a category *"family status"* which relates to the position of the families of husband and wife as assessed by village assistants and key informants.

We suggest how relations differ by craft, and specify those relations which limit mobility in land, credit, and labour. Restraints on commoditisation (i.e. translating intangibles into commodities) are noted. Relations in rural or semi-rural areas in subsistence, traditional, and tourist crafts are different from those in highly industrialised urban areas where fully capitalised production takes place. We hope especially to note these differences for women.

We discuss the position of women vis-à-vis men in the process of commoditisation and capitalisation. We believe the aims and attitudes of women differ somewhat from those of men, and that capitalist development affects women differently from men. This difference is often neglected in theories of capitalist development. It has been observed that the relative equality of women and men in various spheres changes at different rates. For this reason and because of other difficulties in cross-cultural comparisons in the women's position alone (Oppong, 1980), it has been suggested that understanding the position of women in a given culture vis-à-vis men in the same culture may be the most appropriate way of defining status for women. We have accepted this assumption in our study.

The study is relevant to the need for education and skills to equip women in lower income groups for a role in national development. Education and training for these women, who have hitherto been somewhat overlooked by government training policies, if combined with co-operatives and credit schemes, may provide ways for women in these groups to increase income-generating skills, life chances, and socio-economic conditions. Results of such programmes would certainly be reflected in family behaviour in general and parental roles in particular.

Notes
1) See Goldschmidt-Clermont 1982. The Association of Social Anthropologists meeting (1979) on the topic of work also pointed to the lack of sufficient attention to this area as one of the pressing problems in anthropology.

II.   THE SOCIAL ENVIRONMENT: KERDASSA

The community

Kerdassa, the second largest community in Giza governorate, lies 15 kilometres south-west of Cairo, and 6 kilometres northwest of the Giza pyramids. The pyramids dominate the landscape on a clear day and provide the reason for the growing tourist industry in the village.

Historically, Kerdassa was not known as an agricultural village but rather as a village specialising in various handicrafts. Although no written records of its history exist, older residents recount its prominence as a weaving centre, where most of its residents were at one time employed on handlooms. Merchant families of several generations still ply the trade founded by their forebears when Kerdassa was a prominent stop on the desert routes to Tunisia and the Libyan Arab Jamahiriya. A south-bound trade with Sudan and Chad also flourished and the town still keeps old trading contacts with both eastern and western desert areas, with the Libyan Arab Jamahiriya and with oases such as Siwa, offering textiles and rugs from these areas to the burgeoning tourist trade.

The town surrounds the egg-shaped nucleus of the original settlement which stood above the flood plain and which, since the first Aswan dam at the turn of the century, has encroached onto the flood plain. Lush green agricultural land and date palms surround the town, with its narrow streets and close-built houses. Pathways strewn with rubbish, waste water and animal refuse greatly contrast with the cleaner and more open area surrounding it.

At the entrance to the town, farthest from the pyramids, there lies a strip of "bazaars" which have grown in number from two in 1972 to the present 51, in response to increased tourism. In the past few years many new shops have been opened by merchants from the old bazaar area in Cairo, and this has formed a dichotomy of insiders/outsiders, as local handwoven textiles are more and more supplemented with other bazaar craft products manufactured outside the village.

At least four-fifths of the residents are landless and so must find work in or outside the village, or in the small factories which have sprung up around Giza. The rest farm their own land, rent, or sharecrop. The minority work in skilled trades, professional fields, or the nearby government offices. Many small-scale industries may be viewed along the main streets and home industries can be seen when wandering along the side roads.

The population

The official Government Census of 1976 provided an estimate of 29,361 residents; 14,294 females and 15,067 males. A survey carried out in 1979 by the government census bureau gave a figure of 32,303, which suggests an annual growth rate of 3.23 per cent. The Governorate of Giza suggests a current figure of 52,000,

7

which fits the villagers' estimates fairly accurately. The ethnic composition of Kerdassa is homogeneous and the religious composition is nearly so. With the exception of a few thousand Coptic Christians the population is Moslem, and 23 mosques and one church dot the village. The culture of the area is expressed largely in Islamic terms and Koranic references, although folk practices and beliefs do exist. Time itself is dominated by the ritual of Islam, as the calls to prayer echoing from mosque to mosque around the village structure activities as well as giving time for reflection.

Migration from Kerdassa is low by Egyptian standards, which may be due to existing employment opportunities. Yet a number of young educated males have travelled to other Middle Eastern countries to work, particularly the Libyan Arab Jamahiriya, returning to settle after they have saved money to marry, an increasingly expensive process. These men come predominantly from merchant and landowning families. It is very rare for women to move away, though some have married in neighbouring villages.

The administration

Kerdassa is governed by town and governorate councils composed of both elected and appointed members for terms of four years. Since 1965 the office of *oumda* (mayor) has been abolished and the head of the town council is appointed from outside the town by the governor of Giza. Both councils are subject to national guidance and control. The governorate maintains a large compound near the entrance to the village adjoining the police station, which is also a branch of the central government. The district and governorate also send representatives to the national parliament (People's Assembly) through participation in the national party.

Kerdassa has an agricultural bank which was recently established to supplement the services of the agricultural co-operatives. Lending policies are quite liberal and 1 000 televisions were financed in Kerdassa last year by the bank. Women can obtain sewing machines only if husbands have established credit with the bank, or they may do this through the Productive Families Unit of the social services centre which is run by the central Ministry of Social Affairs. The Productive Families Unit has been the major supporter of craftsmen throughout Egypt and is willing to lend money to families to buy materials or equipment to begin any sort of small craft business. However, it must first be established by the social worker that this is a "needy" family, and so this is not a system of credit which can be utilised by the general public. The entire budget for this expenditure is only a few thousand pounds for the entire country and it cannot be considered as a large-scale effort by the government to boost small production. Most financing for crafts in the village is unofficial. Women sometimes run revolving credit associations, but these are primarily used for weddings or feasts and not as productive enterprises.

Women generally do not organise in rural Egypt beyond the extended family level, a serious impediment to attempts to further income-generating schemes for women. Women congregate for weddings and funerals, and occasionally visiting, but not for other reasons. In some areas of Egypt, community-based self-help groups have been successful, but generally the lowest income groups who need the most assistance are isolated from information networks and wider organisations, an issue

8

which needs to be highlighted.

A voluntary association has been responsible for organising the raising of funds for local schools, roads, and other projects. This sort of community co-operation for development is characteristic of the village, where well-to-do residents and merchants are expected to support general welfare projects. Women are not represented at the community level and above it, and can only influence decisions on local issues indirectly through family pressure and by appealing to their husbands. Nevertheless, they are not unaware of community interests and are generally positive and forceful in their lives and relationships with others.

Communication

Buses and minibuses connect the area with Giza and Cairo as well as surrounding villages at frequent intervals. Newspapers are readily available from a central kiosk and a cinema is located in the governorate complex. An influx of television sets has brought the outside world into Kerdassa and is responsible for accelerating changing social values. Minibus fares are 12 piastres. Goods can be transported on the roof rack, and market women and merchants often use them to transport goods. A road leading to the central Pyramids Road was surfaced four years ago. Donkey carts also provide transport to surrounding areas. Several residents have telephones which can be used by the public, for a small fee.

Power and sanitation

Nearly all the households in Kerdassa have electricity, which is fed from a transformer located at each side of the village. Because of overloads caused by increased building and use of electrical appliances, the current is constantly cut off, another situation which merchants bemoan. Most houses have only bare bulb lighting in one or two rooms. Very few houses have actual taps or pumps inside the house for water, but rather use public taps scattered at strategic points about the village. Women and girls carry water from these taps to their homes on their heads in large galvanised tins. If a resident has a pump he is expected to share water freely with neighbours. Despite government efforts to supply clean, drinkable water to every village, we constantly see women washing cooking pots, pans and dishes in the canals. We also see women in the fields adjoining canals washing vegetables before marketing them. Some canals are extremely polluted and all carry bilharzia. Unfortunately no television campaigns have been instigated to stem this serious health hazard.

Pit toilets are the predominant form of facility and these are of a public and a private nature. Private homes have pit toilets enclosed in individual stalls or located under stairways. Mosques provide public toilets for males only. Toilets range from ceramic-faced and tiled toilets in middle class homes to simple ceramic squares inset in earth in the majority of homes. Some are connected to a central sewage system and water may be poured down them, but some are only dug out. It is difficult to keep these clean, although cans of water are provided for individual washing, and recent crowding in villages has increased the hazard. Chickens and pigeons may roost above toilets, adding considerably to the bacteria count. Small children defecate in the street or alley

9

in front of their homes. Animals (dogs, donkeys, gamoosa, cows, sheep, goats) and fowl (ducks, chickens, pigeons) also evacuate both in the alley and in the house, although they are usually confined to certain areas. Cats, chickens, pigeons, and wild birds have free run of the house. Men and children may also use outside areas such as roadsides, canal banks and fields for evacuation.

Housekeeping and food handling customs, washing children, and human interaction are geared to cultural ideas of cleanliness, rather than to an understanding of bacterial contamination. For example, rituals of washing after meals are carefully observed, while this is not customary before meals or before food handling. Attempts are made to separate human and animal wastes from food preparation areas but many other practices mitigate against the success of this. As pure water has to be carried sometimes considerable distances, it is used more sparingly and may sometimes become contaminated in transport. Dishes are washed near the doorstep where women squat, stacking pans face down on the earth. Food preparation takes place on the earth floor in the area where clothes are washed and where fowl and animals congregate and where naked young children may be present. Carrying open dishes of food or milk from neighbouring homes or shops is common. All these practices have a direct effect on health and on child survival. Deep-seated cultural ideals and practices are difficult to eradicate, and so far the government has failed to lead any serious campaign against these dangers, believing that the presence of clean water within walking distance is sufficient.

Education

There are three primary schools in Kerdassa and one intermediate school with a few classes for secondary school-aged children. About one-third of the girls finish the first six years of primary school and this figure declines even further in preparatory and secondary schools. We do not have accurate figures for the percentage of eligible children who attend school but we estimate it at approximately two-thirds of primary school-age children. While current illiteracy rates for women in rural areas vary between 74-95 per cent, depending upon area and age (Capmas, 1976; Gadalla, 1978), this is rapidly changing. Currently, however, only upper class women complete secondary schooling, and there are few of these. Attitudes toward education have changed, as evidenced by comments by women about their own lack of education and regrets about daughters who did not attend or did not finish school. Many young girls now take studies seriously, attending extra tutoring sessions regularly, and they have high aspirations. The free education system begun under Nasser has had a great effect on class structure in Egypt and this effect will increase with the current generation. The system allows parents who can afford to support children not contributing to the household income, to keep their children at school. Free schooling must often be supplemented by tutoring, however, as conditions of overcrowding and double and triple sessions mean that children may not pass examinations which determine participation in the next level. Families may also sacrifice to send girls who are good students to secondary school and even university, where this may mean a brother will not be educated. This will increase the woman's chance of making a good marriage, thus increasing the status of the entire family. Nevertheless, as we show in the case studies, not all families are able to educate daughters, even where sons may be at school.

Adoption of conservative Islamic dress and life style is increasing and may be linked with education and status (thus income). Women engaged in crafts tell us they do not wish to be encumbered by the more restrictive veil (*hijab*).

Vocational training as an alternative to education at higher levels is not available in Kerdassa. Boys at upper levels travel to technical training schools in Giza. This training is planned by the central government through the Ministry of Manpower and is exclusively directed at males. The Ministry of Social Affairs runs a small, intermittent training programme through local social centres for female "school-leavers", usually teaching them embroidery. This is not a serious vocational training programme for income generation among rural women; they learn skills which have little relevance to their lives or their basic income needs.

As education is directly related to age at marriage and indirectly to fertility through this and other ways (Loza, 1981), it is a dominant issue. Education has been found to be the single most important means through which changes in fertility have been realised in some areas of Egypt (Ibrahim, 1980), but functional literacy has been insufficient to change attitudes (Gadalla, 1978).

Despite recent changes, the majority of women in Kerdassa remain uneducated and, as functional literacy is the only goal being met at present, we cannot expect favourable change in the near future, either for lower income groups or for all women.

The mosque

Although women do not participate in the practice of religion in public in Egypt, women in Kerdassa take an active role in religious life. Although they do not use the mosque as an important place to exchange information, express social and political solidarity, and for recreation, as men do, women recite the Koran after a death and there are certain women renowned locally for this. Whereas men recite on the first day, women use the microphone to recite on the second day. This can be an impressive sight as large numbers of women congregate to mourn. Predominantly older women observe this custom as younger women with children find it difficult to spend the time. Funeral tents attached to mosques or other public meeting spaces are supplied for men of the community to present their condolences to the male relatives of the deceased whereas women present condolences to female relatives inside and outside the home of the deceased.

Kinship, marriage and law

In rural Egypt marriage is a family concern and is still commonly arranged by parents and or close relatives although the young boy or girl may be consulted on the choice of a partner. Women have less power in decision-making and distribution of resources than men in this patrilineal kinship system. They do not have the choice of a marriage partner as men do, although they have the right to refuse partners. Women's marital and sexual lives are strictly controlled by the male members of the family, and a mother is not anxious to see her daughter's chances for a suitable marriage diminish. High value is placed on chaste, obedient women who are highly fertile and strong. All women are expected to marry before 20 and many in this village still marry

11

under 16, although this is the legal age. Age at marriage is rising,[1,2]however, primarily due to rising education levels and the high cost of *mahr*, or bridewealth[3].

When a woman becomes engaged (*shabkat*) an agreed sum is paid to her by the groom's family, after this has been settled between the two sets of parents. This money is used to buy gold for the prospective bride or copper objects for the household. The woman keeps the gold but may later be asked to sell some of it if her husband needs money. She is not expected to refuse. Although by law a marriage contract often has "arrears" to be paid on divorce, in practice this money is seldom collected by divorced women.

It is the bride's family's obligation to purchase furnishings for the home of the new couple and they do this with the *mahr*, recording the amount spent. If the man divorces her she is entitled to the furnishings, but if she leaves her husband she is sometimes unable to collect it. Other gifts of food, animals, and basic necessities sent to the new household by the bride's family are called *el Asr*.

Virilocality is the rule, although an increasing number of new couples have their own home. Endogamy is practiced in the village, and patrilineal cousin marriage (FBD) is still preferred. However, many cousins fit into this category, as all male relatives on the father's side who are older than the groom are called *amm* (uncle).

Marrying within the village is preferred and informants tell us that no woman marries outside unless she has not received a good offer within the village. Mothers have a prominent role in choosing a bride for their sons as they are in a position to gain more information about the qualities of a prospective wife. Women also prefer to marry their daughter locally.

Women are expected to bear many children and sons are very highly favoured. If a woman bears few children, her husband may take a second wife or divorce her. Limited polygamy is present, especially among lower income groups, but only men are allowed multiple spouses. A first wife may refuse to live with a new wife and may divorce her husband if she does not accept the second marriage. Culturally, however, she is expected to allow this and to co-operate with the new wife, and is thought troublesome if she does not. In some cases women prefer to co-operate with co-wives for their mutual benefit. In the cases of Safeya and Hamida we show examples of this co-operation which allows considerable freedom to women active in production and marketing.

Family law in Egypt is based on religious law (*Shari'a*). Under this law women had until recently, limited legal grounds to divorce a husband against his wishes and these were often difficult to implement, whereas he, according to ancient folklore, could divorce her simply by making a verbal statement of this three times. In fact the civil court at present makes divorce extremely difficult. Until recently, a woman who divorced her husband forfeited her right to support; otherwise he was obliged to support her for one year. A recent law has allowed a woman who wishes to divorce one year's support for every five years of marriage and rights to permanent occupancy of the family home. Children legally belong to the family of the husband after the age of nine for a girl and seven for a boy. Husbands have full authority and final decision-making power over wives, including the right to inflict physical punishment, although there are differences of opinion on this subject. Men often express a belief that women are not morally as strong as men and need to be "guided", although, here again, differences arise.

A high value is placed on males who are aggressive, strong, and sexually potent, but patience, wisdom, and gentleness are also prized. While there are some tendencies within local interpretations of Islam, especially by religious males, to regard female sexual power as contaminating to men and tending to lead them away from the correct life, women are greatly valued for their beauty, their sexual attraction, and for their nurturing warmth. Society is sexually segregated outside the extended family, although this is diminishing. There is a strong obligation for women to obey their husbands, to perform domestic tasks for them, and to turn their money over to them if they sell produce from the household unit.

A women has a right to inherit half as much as a man and to pass her property on to her children, but sometimes it is observed that a woman cannot claim her inheritance and it passes to her brothers. A woman retains the name of her father after marriage and her daughters take the name of their father. A husband is expected to provide basic support for his wife and if he does not she may appeal to other male members of his family for help. All of these values are enforced with passages from the Koran, which support the social order, according to specific local interpretations.

Medical care and family planning

The governorate maintains an outpatient clinic within its compound with a staff of two physicians and a nurse-midwife (*hakima*) for several hours each morning (9 a.m.–2 p.m.), treating patients for 10 piastres (10 piastres = 15 cents American) a visit. A programme for the Population and Development Project is administered through this clinic. Five female leaders (*ra'idaa rifia*) were appointed by the local council to augment this project on a household level, making visits to pregnant women and those recently delivered, in the hope of influencing them in adopting family planning methods. We agree with the doubts expressed by the Population and Family Planning Board as to whether these women represent the village as a whole or whether they are from a privileged group. There is also a problem with the motivation of the female leaders, probably due to the low remuneration which they receive. Women with sick children often have a long wait, and the same is true if they visit for family planning, advice, or medication. Our informants also told us that some doctors run private clinics on government property in the afternoons and sell medications which have been supplied for free distribution to village residents.

The village contains 25 private health clinics (according to informants), some run by village doctors who are very committed to their patients. However, poorer residents often cannot afford the Egyptian pounds (LE)1 fee. Many residents are aware of hospital facilities and outpatient clinics in Giza and in Cairo where they can go for health problems, X-rays, or emergencies, often free of charge. There are about four *dayas* (traditional midwives) in the village who are untrained but who deliver most babies. We think it is unfortunate that efforts under Nasser to bring *dayas* under the medical system by training them in the basic techniques of delivery and sanitation, were eventually abandoned. Village doctors told us that *dayas* will seek their assistance only when they face a difficult delivery. They claim that certain cultural practices which are dangerous to mothers are practised by *dayas*, such as encouraging mothers to hasten births by straining over long periods. This may promote both pre- and post-partum haemorrhage, which can result in the death of the

13

mother, or which otherwise weakens her. This accusation is not borne out by statistics. Only about 1 per cent of mothers died in childbirth, which, as many local women marry between 13 and 18 years of age, is very low. It is not, however, uncommon for first or even second babies to die soon after birth or to be stillborn. Female mortality exceeds that of males in Egypt, and together with infant mortality is disguised or under-reported (Nour, 1979).

Infant mortality rates in urbanised villages in Giza are among the highest in Egypt (CAPMAS Census 1967 in Loza, 1980) and gastro-enteritis may be responsible for this. The major health problem for adults is malnutrition and its many effects, and bilharzia which also still affects 75 per cent of the children and which is responsible for a high rate of chronic renal infection and urinary tract cancer between the ages of 35-40. Abortion, while not common, is practised. As it is illegal it is especially difficult for low income women to find clinics which will perform abortions they could afford. Folk methods are dangerous and painful and involve insertion of a foreign body into the uterus, usually a stem from a common local green plant, then binding the abdomen tightly, thus forming pressure from both ends. It is usually effective, but resulting haemorrhage may cause death. Most women in the village have no antenatal or post-natal care and many do not recognise the need for it.

There is at least one dentist in the village. The four pharmacies are conveniently located and sell birth control pills for 5 piastres for a month's supply, the same price as in the government clinic.

While we were in the village, a programme for vaccination of children between the ages of 1 and 4 was being carried out by the two clinic nurses who are also responsible for post-natal care for mothers and babies at home. In a village of 52,000 one can see the problem in expecting them to fulfil all these needs.

The household

In existing studies, the focus has long been the household, which was considered a homogeneous unit with undifferentiated interests. Economists and demographers have recently realised that this assumption is inadequate (Long and Richardson, 1980, pp. 158-184). Women are a special case; they do not labour under the same conditions as men and are not affected by development in the same way. Decision-making power and distribution of resources may differ across lines of sex, age, and the life cycle of the household unit. Relations between the sexes have been found to affect the outcome of externally-directed family planning policies, as well.

Sex, age, life and family cycle differences can only be understood by defining the total participation of individual members of the household and by taking into consideration the context within which each individual works. Youssef (1974, p. 24) has accurately called for the definition of changes from wider economic pressures upon household "flow of relations" and for a like definition of changes from within the household patterns upon fertility attitudes and behaviour. She suggests that fertility may be a response to a heavy workload and therefore female relationships with other females are important as well as those with males. Such changes may not be evident until individual participation is well defined according to a much wider set of criteria than those now present in the data.

14

Studies which cover all aspects of women's lives are essential to provide the understanding needed to plan for women's position in future development through work. In defining household responsibility for tasks, it may be determined which activities, in particular cultural contexts, are elastic and which are not, or under what circumstances they may become so (Mueller in Anker, Buvinic and Youssef, 1982). From this type of in-depth contextual study we may also determine what patterns in the sex based division of labour are associated with a high preference for children and which groups of activity are related to kinds of reproductive behaviour and attitudes (Youssef, 1974, p. 24).

The rise of merchant and commercial capital may increase the need for women to produce more labourers and diminish their involvement in other social roles (Youssef, 1974, p. 27). This can best be determined by examining the social participation of women. An internal family hierarchy and narrower division of labour, favouring males, also affects female influence in decision-making including fertility decisions (Youssef, 1974, p. 27). Failure of government attempts to implement family planning programmes may have some relation to lack of consideration of these issues.

Food preparation and diet

Women play an important role in food provision as well as preparation at all levels, with contributions ranging in many cases right from garden to table. Women often harvest crops, transport them from the field, process them, then prepare and cook them. Bread making, date preparation, and corn husking are common to most households, although by no means inclusive of all the time-consuming tasks executed by women. The coarse, delicious light brown flat loaf, which forms the diet staple, is baked once or twice a week by most of the women in our study. Wheat is purchased in the market and is ground locally. The process of sifting, mixing, forming, and baking is very labour intensive and takes the major part of an evening and morning. It is often done in groups based on the extended family so as to conserve fuel, and neighbours may also share an oven or use a public *furn* which serves their street. Corn husking and date preparation are equally time consuming, and like all food preparation, require almost no equipment. Considerable skill is, however, necessary for these tasks.

Kerosene is utilised in the *babour*. It is subsidised by the government and therefore costs only 4 piastres per litre. It is perhaps the most essential housekeeping item. Women supply other cooking fuel. The environment dictates that wood cannot be used for fuel so women gather dry kindling from palm groves or from the fields and can be seen carrying huge loads on their heads from areas surrounding the town. This task is mainly assigned to young, unmarried women and girls. Very young girls from 7 to 10 collect dung from the streets and marketplace and mix this with straw to make cakes of *gella* for the clay oven. If a household has no small daughters to do this women may make *gella* themselves, or may purchase it for 30 piastres per hundred.

The combination of the presence of Nile mud from former floods, Nile water, and a warm climate with plenty of sun, make the Egyptian delta and adjoining areas a fertile environment. Continuous fresh vegetables and extremely long fruit seasons combine to give variety to the diet, dates grow moist and plump on the many palms, and animals reproduce more than once a year as in more moderate climates. In spite of these bounteous blessings from Mother Nature, the primary health hazard in Kerdassa is malnutrition.

15

The interesting and varied diet masks certain basic deficiencies which must be kept in mind. The diet, especially for lower income groups, revolves about grain staples such as breads and grain-based main dishes, supplemented with legumes. It is partially in the method of serving and eating food that diet deficiencies are promoted. It is not that essential foods are not present, but that in communal dishes they are not consumed in sufficient quantity to ensure a well regulated diet. We also note that several fairly recent changes in dietary habits have especially affected the protein intake of lower income groups. Although it is generally believed that meat consumption has risen in recent times and that it is available to more of the population, we found that this depended on income. Kerdassans eat camel and fowl and rarely fish, and usually consume meat not more than twice a week, although poorer families may eat meat only rarely.

In the past, corn and wheat formed a basic staple of the Egyptian diet. Combined with broad beans (*fool*), another staple food, it formed a complete protein. Neither beans nor grain alone contain the seven amino acids necessary to qualify as a source of protein. But now corn is used less than before, as use of *bitau* (corn bread) and corn starch has diminished. Although wheat is still used, purchase of ready-baked bread has increased, and this uses subsidised, bleached flour. There is also, as in most parts of the world, an alarming increase of sugar in the diet. The Egyptian diet was not previously rich in refined sugars but with the change to modern food habits, natural drinks such as fruit juices, *tamrahinde, karkade* (a drink from flower blossoms), and fresh sugar juice from cane are being replaced by carbonated soft drinks and sugar syrup drinks. Healthy snacks such as fruit, seeds, and nuts are still present but cheap sugar sweets are also being increasingly offered to children as well as adults.

Most families in Kerdassa eat three meals per day. Breakfast (*al futuur*) is served soon after rising, usually about 8 a.m., lunch (*al ghada*) is eaten between 2 p.m. and 3 p.m. and is the main meal of the day, and dinner (*al 'asha*) is served around 7 p.m. It is very important for the family to eat meals together and they are a time of relaxation and communication as well as of taking nourishment. Deep cultural values surrounding generosity and hospitality define food preparation and serving. No visitor is ever to be turned away hungry and any extended family member present during mealtime must be fed. Women must transport meals to working husbands, brothers, or fathers in the fields or in other parts of the village and must provide cooked food for employed construction workers, craft workers, or apprentices. Women are expected to reheat and serve meals for any late-comers. Sick relatives or aged parents must be provided for. No feast or ritual is celebrated without a communal meal. Women often cook and serve together, a time which they use for chatting and exchanging information.

The following examples give an idea of the women's obligation to prepare and provide food: a daughter or cousin is expected to assist her mother (or aunt) in meeting a son's obligations to entertain his friends, even if she has her own family and lives elsewhere; mothers, sisters, and wives must entertain friends of males on request; a brother can send guests unannounced to his sister and she must serve them graciously and uncomplainingly as she would her husband; during the great feast of Ramadan entire families may visit every day to be entertained and fed; food is distributed on the street whenever a new child is born, circumcised, engaged, married; a daughter shares produce and cooked food with her mother and mother's family if she needs it.

Laundry

Like cooking, laundry is a distinctly sex-linked task. As water must sometimes be carried considerable distances, this can be a heavy job, especially before daughters are old enough to assist with this task. Each garment is soaked and scrubbed by hand, then rinsed and placed on the roof to dry. Several trips are necessary to complete the several rinses needed, and waste water must then be transported to specified areas of the village for disposal. Because this is heavy work, some women throw bath, waste, and cooking water in to the street or the canal, which contributes heavily to pollution. As clothes are very important and are well cared for, laundries are large and frequent. Women may have to climb unsafe ladders to reach the drying area. Ironing is not usually done at home, but those few garments which require it are sent to the neighbourhood *makwagi* (ironer).

House cleaning

Women usually rise early to sweep and tidy the house before breakfast and to feed animals and fowl. This task is done perhaps several times during the day, and especially before the family meal in the evening. As many floors are packed earth they are not washed, and a simple hand whisk made of palm fibre is used for sweeping. Both this and the stiff date branch broom require a woman to bend over while sweeping. This task is made more difficult as refuse is not collected in one place by household residents but rather thrown onto the floor or left there from activities taking place. For craftswomen working at home or for wives of craftsmen this can be a time consuming duty.

Child-care

No other single activity makes more demands upon the time and energy of women than child-care. In addition to purely physical demands involved in the reproduction and meeting of material needs of large families, Egyptian culture places great value on the quality of family life. Indeed, no other benefits in life are thought to replace in any way those to be gained from domestic life, and domestic life means children. A woman's relation to child-care varies over her life cycle, and throughout her life she is involved in more than a peripheral way.

In Kerdassa children are not just considered another mouth to feed, but are the wellspring of joy for all members of the extended family and even for outsiders. What would be considered extreme patience by westerners may not be looked upon in the same way by Egyptians. Men, as well as women, are directly involved in the care and teaching of children, and uncles and older siblings dote on them. From birth until 4 or 5 years old, when they begin to assist about the house, children are pampered and loved by everyone.

What does this mean to women directly? Firstly, we have observed in our case studies and throughout the village a fundamental difference in the care and feeding of young infants from urban Egyptian or western practices. Infants are breastfed on demand and are carried about all the time by their mothers, whilst the latter carry out their task. If the mother is not holding the baby, she passes it to another family member.

Infants are not only breastfed for nourishment, but for pacification, and this usually continues for two years[4]. Introduction of solid foods is slow, so babies make great demands upon mothers at the age of four or five months. This is vital, as recent research on prolactin has shown that even malnourished mothers will produce milk at the expense of their own bones, teeth, and general health. Prolactin levels adjust to the baby's need, not to that of the mother. African investigations have also shown that undernourished mothers will be infertile while breastfeeding. If properly nourished, women may be fertile during this period.

As Egyptian women bear large numbers of children and lose a high percentage by world standards, they spend a great deal of time and physical resources on bearing, feeding and caring for infants. The demands of this process cannot be overestimated, especially under the present poor conditions for pre- and post-natal care.

Mothers are allowed and expected to feed infants at any time or place. In recognition of the importance of this role, garments are designed to facilitate this in public.

The high rate of infant and child mortality is believed to affect attitudes toward childbearing in Egypt[5] and to increase the desire for large families. Social nurturing roles are stressed to ensure survival of as many children as possible, and high demands for child-care do not cease with infancy. A woman is expected to devote herself to this care and to insure the co-operation of women of all ages. While men also value children and teach and watch them, it is primarily the duty of women to guard against health hazards, to insure emotional security, and to keep children clothed and fed. It is the mother's obligation to provide food for the children even after they are adult, and other work roles do not interfere with this function. Wherever women exist, and where they congregate, we can observe them feeding and caring for children.

We see that in rural households women help to grow, harvest and process many of the subsistence needs. They purchase basic foods, feed and care for all animals and fowl and provide secondary animal products for the table. Women bear, feed and nurture the children in a manner which has changed little in thousands of years. The female contribution to subsistence is, therefore, important and is expanded in specific instances to include a significant productive role in activities beyond subsistence needs.

Notes
1) Gadalla shows that, although the average age at marriage for women in his survey is 15.9 for rural women of 45-49 years, the median age at marriage has risen in villages in his study during the past 30 years from as low as 14.9 to as high as 18.4. Age and area differences, therefore, cannot be ignored, but the general trend is to a later age at marriage, usually 17 or over (Gadalla, 1978, p. 77-8).
2) Loza shows in her study that the average age at marriage is between 15.9 and 18.5 depending upon rural or urban setting, and that the percentage of marriage under 17 in rural areas is often 30-50 per cent (Loza, 1981, Table A.4.6, p. 150).

3) We term *mahr* here as bridewealth which is passed from the family of the groom to that of the bride, and which forms a fund. Actually, *mahr* is "indirect dowry" of the type called by Goody "diverging devolution", that is, part of a "familial or conjugal fund which is passed from holder to heir". In this case funds are paid from the groom's family to the bride through her father and are matched by funds or movable property from the bride's parents to the bride, although many complain that grooms now assume a much larger portion. It is meant to establish a new household, and is called locally "dowry" (J. Goody, 1973, p. 17).

4) Gadalla notes that most village women in Egypt accept the wisdom of nursing for two years, as suggested in the Koran (Gadalla, 1978, p. 159). Loza found a mean lactation duration of 21.2 months in rural areas in her study (Loza, 1981, p. 95, Table 5.8).

5) Nour (1979) notes that infant deaths account for nearly 50 per cent of all deaths in Egypt.

III.   THE ECONOMIC CONTEXT

Land, labour and industry

Land reform measures brought about by the Nasser regime since 1952 have helped to redistribute landholdings to some extent, although mostly benefitting medium-sized landowners and not the landless poor. This has had the effect of hastening the division of property generally so that at present the largest group of landowners (97.5 per cent of all farmers) comprises farmers holding less than 5 *feddans*[1]. If we look at all the households in Kerdassa, we find that:

    270 families own less than 1 *feddan*
    960 families own 1–3 *feddans*
    11 families own 4–9 *feddans*
    20 families own over 10 *feddans*.

Assuming the population figure from governorate estimates (52,000) and assuming five persons per household, we know there are approximately 10,500 households in Kerdassa, of which 9,239 or 88 per cent do not own any land. Not all the landowners are farmers. Some rent out land or let it in a sharecropping arrangement and smallholders may also rent in or sharecrop the land of others in addition to their own. Whether land is rented out or not depends primarily on the family composition (number and type of available labour) and on the stage in the family life cycle (for example, whether the family is made up of a young married couple with small children, a middle aged couple with adolescent or grown children, or an older couple, a widowed or divorced person with married children).

Land has a high value in the area because of its proximity to the city, because of growing tourism, and because of population expansion. Prime location or fertile land may cost as much as LE 3,000 per *kirat*. Some farmers have indicated that the only use of land now is "to sell it", but others benefit from the exemption of this area from cotton growing, and they can make a profit raising vegetables for the city.

There is a scarcity of agricultural labour in Kerdassa and the day rate quoted for workers is LE 2, which is higher than the LE 1 usual in Beni Suef, a governorate to the south, and in other areas of Egypt. Five to seven years ago the rate was 25 piastres per day (1 piastre = 1½ cents American).

The location near urban areas gives direct access to an expanded job market. The proximity of several factories, specifically a television and radio assembly plant, a cigarette factory, and an auto assembly plant, provides access to work for many young males mostly at semi-skilled levels, with some overtime and fringe benefits. Tourism provides seasonal service jobs and construction work of a less permanent but currently active nature. Transport jobs are the highest paid in the area but drivers are often required to pay for repairs and fuel and must raise capital for a truck. Those employed in government work in Giza and Cairo are badly paid. Those in professions fare better, but account for a very small percentage of the

21

workforce. Building trades are in special demand in Kerdassa and command LE 5–6 per day plus luncheon. Related skills, which are in short supply due to migration, may command LE 100 per month (carpenters, plumbers, electricians, blacksmiths). These are in demand because of the building boom in local urban areas. Skilled tradesmen, including mechanics, may work in industry in the morning and freelance within the village in the afternoon and evening.

Opportunities for women are less varied than for men and those existing are generally unacceptable because of social restrictions on female mobility.

A small minority of women is employed in medicine, engineering, teaching or nursing and they may travel to the city to work. Because of the very small number of local women with higher education or training, most female teachers travel into Kerdassa from other urban areas. The local urban bureaucracy employs another small group of educated women.

Very few women work in industry outside the village, although this is slowly beginning to change and young unmarried females are joining the factory labour force in order to earn money to marry. Generally a woman, especially an unmarried one, who travels alone to and from the city and who returns home after dark in the short winter days may be the subject of unfavourable gossip. Villagers on the whole do not want to diminish their daughters' chances in the marriage market, and as this has a much higher priority than work, they do not favour employment outside the village for young women. A few married women do work outside, but this is also difficult because of childbearing expectations and the necessity for another woman in the household to assume domestic responsibilities.

Few women are educated or trained for skilled jobs, but those who succeed have more mobility because of the status these jobs bring. For lower income, illiterate, and unskilled women (the vast majority) there is no opportunity to work inside or outside the village except in household industries, cottage industries, handicrafts, and in petty trade. The vast majority of women who need to earn income become traders in vegetables, fowl, or small manufactured commodities. Two local women own and operate tourist shops, but are having trouble competing with more experienced merchants from the city. Other women may invest money in the local tourist industry as "silent partners".

Kerdassa is an area of expanding employment, especially if compared to most rural areas of Egypt. It has a history of specialisation in handicrafts and a much higher than average availability of skills. In this way it is not representative of rural Egypt as a whole. Despite its unusual growth potential, we show in this study that women are unable to find the income-producing work they need. This is even more true for women in other rural areas.

Because there are few opportunities in the village especially for lower income groups, women congregate in those areas which do exist and in this way compete with each other, driving the price of their labour very low (Boserup, 1970). Inflationary pressures, which particularly affect this group, and raised expectations of living standards encourage these women to work for cash which their families require. The fact that they are willing to expend so much effort for such a small return, a fact which we document, proves their need to work and their need for cash to supplement the family income.

22

Agriculture

Although Kerdassans do not describe the town as primarily an agricultural one, it benefits from being in a zone exempted from compulsory cotton production. Farmers here are able to make considerable profits by supplying vegetables to the nearby urban areas of Giza and Cairo.

The important local crops are wheat, corn, dates, citrus fruits (oranges, tangerines, lemons), mangoes, potatoes, cabbage, tomatoes, greens and animal fodder (*bersim*). Men are mostly responsible for planting, hoeing, transplanting, weeding, and ploughing crops while women plant, harvest and help with hoeing and weeding. Women are responsible also for the care of animals, including feeding them and taking them back and forth to pasture every day. Women alone milk cows in Egypt and distribute animal products, which they also prepare. Animals and fowl which are kept in the house are the responsibility of the women. Men market buffalo, cows, goats, donkeys and sheep which women have raised, while women sell chickens, fowl, and eggs. Either men or women may shear sheep and sell wool, but women clean (card) wool and spin it.

Since the advent of perennial irrigation, continuous farming is possible and the climate is favourable. Two major crops may be planted each year and vegetables are planted between times. Produce is marketed in three ways: by large truckers, through small wholesale markets (*tsuega*) who buy directly from producers and sell to city merchants, and through the weekly and daily street markets. Unofficial (local) marketing is done almost entirely by women, whereas the more organised cash crop activities are run solely by men. Grain circulates only through the weekly *suq* which is connected to a rotating market system involving several villages around Kerdassa, each village having its *suq* on a specific day.

Technology levels are extremely low and farming is highly labour intensive especially for smallholders, who form a majority. There are four tractors in the village and irrigation motors may be rented or owned. The short-handled hoe (*fas*) and simple plough (*mahrat*) still form the primary farming implements for these smallholders, as they did in Ancient Egypt. Extreme subdivision of land has placed more importance on the use of (free) family labour than in the past, especially female and child labour because smallholders cannot afford to engage labour, and migration patterns have accentuated this (Harik, 1979).

Currently, the production of fowl and eggs, which form an important part of the local diet and which were always the responsibility of women, is being commercialised by males. As women do not have the available capital, mobility, or networks outside the village to compete with entrepreneurs, they are forced to purchase chickens from new farms for resale in the market at a smaller profit.

Crafts

Recent improvements in communications and growth in tourism have allowed Kerdassans to build upon traditional skills which served city and export markets in weaving products until the village became an important tourist stop. The major products which the village contributes are woven tapestry rugs, locally known as

"Goblan" after the famous French tapestries, *galabeyas* of all description for men and women, and appliqué work. Older, more traditional woven products such as cotton, rayon, and wool shawls and handloomed yarn-goods, and simple woollen *kelims* and blankets are also sold in the shops, especially those of the village merchants.

In addition, there are basket makers who serve numerous surrounding village markets, copper- and blacksmiths working as they have done for many centuries, palm fibre industries, grass-mat manufacturers, and split-palm workers (*gereed*). Carpenters and more modern blacksmiths, ironers, repairmen and mechanics operate from tiny shops which dot the village main streets. Our interest in this study is confined to three categories of handicraft: *traditional* handicrafts of weaving, *versalia*, and tailoring female *galabeyas; tourist* handicrafts of *galabeya* manufacture, tapestry weaving, and embroidery; and *subsistence* handicrafts of basketmaking, straw mat weaving, and blacksmithing. We investigate the role which women, especially, play in the production of some of these goods. Those women who have assumed productive roles in handicrafts in addition to ordinary household duties represent about 10 per cent of all village women. We shall see how they do this in different crafts and in different status groups (see cases, Appendix II). The women chosen as case studies in no way represent all the women in the village, but have been chosen because, at the same time, they are not unusual.

Crafts form an optional income-producing activity for various types of person, such as:

1) kin of second generation (or more) craft families;
2) landless families;
3) lower income and status group families, those lacking education, capital, skills, assets, or connections;
4) families who lack ability to compete for jobs in more sophisticated industries;
5) "surplus" labour (women, older men, children) from households engaged in other occupations;
6) relatives of village merchants;
7) trained or educated males who fail to find work;
8) employed males seeking part-time work.

We show, through case descriptions of craft families and through a discussion of each craft, how life choices differ for households and individuals depending on resources available, family status, family structure, and family life cycle. Social and economic changes are taking place and these may be observed in the choices of second generation craft producers and in the sexual division of labour (see Amina's case). Households with alternative sources of income from land or from employment in modern industry or bureaucracy may have possibilities which do not appear in less advantaged households (see the cases of Amal and Jihan). Modern pressures have far-reaching social implications for the households of the most traditional crafts producers, such as the blacksmith and the weaver (see the cases of Hamida and Amina).

In addition to crafts which formed traditional occupational groups, some households are responding to current demand created by new product uses, by product adaptation, and by growing tourism (see the cases of Safeya, Samira and Nagua). These households may be comprised of the uneducated, untrained, poorer segments of society or surplus labour from more advantaged households who could not find jobs for which they were educated. Some may even be members of landowning families who prefer entrepreneurial activities to farming or who may carry out modern craft activities (see Jihan's case). Merchant households usually recruit labourers for textile and weaving from relatives or from wives of employees (see Halima's case). We show the restrictions of labour mobility on these craft producers.

Surplus labourers from poorer households seek income especially in less skilled crafts such as date palm or reed industries, rope making, mat making, or basket making (see the cases of Nasara, Maryam and Nafisa). These women may participate in crafts voluntarily to earn money needed by their families but more usually are expected to participate because of their role as wife or kin.

Traditional crafts

Weaving

Egyptian villages and towns have been noted for weaving since Pharaonic times, that is, for over 2 000 years. No written history of weaving in Kerdassa exists, but it is believed that this was a speciality which in the past employed most of the residents. A small amount of traditional textiles have been manufactured here for many years for rural and Bedouin communities in the Republic of Tunisia, the Libyan Arab Jamahiriya, the Democratic Republic of the Sudan and Siwa oasis, which, together with Cairo, comprised major markets for local products. A number of workshops which are now unused and in disrepair also mark the present decline in the handloom weaving industry.

In spite of this, there are small workshops throughout the village producing wool, cotton, rayon and synthetic products, rugs, and tapestries. There are some differences in both the workshop organisation and the market orientation of these diverse products. Local cotton, rayon, and synthetic weaving is dominated by one merchant, the younger representative of a prominent clan of textile merchants who ran the southern and western trade in the past. Whilst three of his uncles are still alive, only one is in competition with him. Many small workshops and homes supply outlets for this merchant and these enjoy a prominent location in the main street, which draws most of the tourist trade to the village. The merchant also employs a large number of tailors of *galabeyas* for women and men, and runs an extensive cottage industry for decorating these *galabeyas*.

Most of the looms producing cloth for this family business are owned by the merchant, who provides raw materials and an expert to warp the looms for weavers. Manual *jacquard*, four-post, and tapestry looms of both throw-shuttle and fly-shuttle varieties are employed in the workshops. Weavers are paid only for their labour, at a small rate based on production. Some work in his workshops and some live in his houses. Under present labour conditions a monopoly which the family may have had no longer exists, but links to producers are numerous and include kinship as well as supplier/client relationships. The merchant spends a great deal of time, effort, and money retaining and solidifying relations with producers in the village, in the western desert, and in Sharkeya province, where Bedouin women weave *kelims* and other products. His interest in the village and the weavers goes beyond pure profit motivation, although he uses ownership of production means and kinship relations to

25

exploit producers by keeping wages very low. With the influx of many merchants from outside, conditions have not improved, as competition increases.

A quite separate cotton weaving industry exists which occupies weavers who work simple pit-looms (*nol al ard*) in their own household workshops. These weavers were prominent in the oldest area of the village, where they still congregate, but very few younger weavers exist in this craft nowadays. Mostly they are older weavers who have done this work all their lives and who produce hand towels and check head-wraps, heavy cloths for cleaning, and netting fabrics like *versalia* and shroud-cloth. These weavers are skilled and know how to adjust and adapt their own looms. They cling to this unremunerative craft because they like it, because their identity is very closely linked with their work, and because they do not know any other work.

These weavers are also merchant-dominated, and while most of them own their own looms, they purchase raw materials from merchants and sell finished products back to them for a rate (*hitta*) based on production per metre. Some travel to the old bazaar area in Cairo to sell products. Despite the superior quality of their products, which allows them to retain a small market, they do not compete with machine-made and imported products.

When a weaver works at home his wife is expected to dye cotton and to wind bobbins for her husband, and his production depends on her preparation. All fees which the weaver receives for his labour include his wife's unpaid labour. If a weaver is forced to hire women from outside to wind bobbins in their own homes, he pays for this work at a very low rate which is equivalent to 37 cents per day. If a weaver works in a workshop rather than at home, male apprentices are hired to do peripheral jobs. There is a taboo against the use of foot-pedal looms by women, and so women in Egypt do not weave on these looms and are not employed in workshops.

Independent wool weavers, who weave a variety of products not covered in the study, may be better paid than cotton weavers, and some of them also work as merchants and middlemen. Some merchants do not produce, as they consider it beneath their status to do so. Cultural values have long supported this view. As soon as a man becomes a merchant who does not produce, his wife no longer maintains a productive role in subsidiary activities; she feels that, because of her economic position, winding bobbins, spinning, or dyeing are unfit work for her.

There is a small cottage industry in wool spinning, although this is dying out despite the presence of many herds. Spun wool is now purchased mostly from public sector spinning mills, from specialist villages, or from city merchants who have imported it. Those remaining in wool spinning are mostly older women who earn between 15 and 60 cents per day.

Versalia

Though the women's role in production is a peripheral one in weaving, it is central to the production of *versalia*. This is a very stiff fabric which comes in many grades and which is used as a lining material in luggage, handbags, and clothing. About 15 years ago cotton weavers and cloth merchants in the village moved to this industry to fill the needs of the growing ready-to-wear clothing and luggage markets in Cairo and to escape their declining craft. Production is organised by merchants linked to small producers in the old bazaar area and the "Muski" in Cairo. Women's labour is heavily utilised in *versalia*. Women work within the household and are organised by male household heads. Women are not paid for this work, although it is heavy, dirty, and time consuming. Household composition and structure determine internal distribution of tasks in production, and our case study shows how one polygamous household takes advantage of an abundance of female labour to run a lucrative business (see Safeya's case). Unlike most of the handicrafts in Kerdassa, this business is not seasonal and has a steady demand and organised outlets. It is a good example of how traditional skills, both productive and managerial, can be utilised in more modern industries.

Tailoring of traditional dresses

We have termed the production of the customary dress for women in the village a "traditional" handicraft because of its cultural significance and its long existence. This is the only "monopoly" which women have retained in Kerdassa — women produce all the clothing for local women. Local estimates of the number of women employed as tailors have reached 200, a not unreasonable figure in a population of 50,000. Women own their own sewing machines and customers bring fabrics to them to be made up into *galabeyas*, which are then decorated by the tailor, by other women who do hand-beading only, or by men who specialise in machine-embroidering the yoke in colourful local designs. Women, who generally lack mobility outside the village, do not monopolise the sale of fabric, although there are a few cloth merchants who are women. The imported beads traditionally used to decorate the yoke are also brought into the village by men and sold to women. As finishing is shared by men and men control raw materials, the monopoly is certainly not total.

Women in Kerdassa dress noticeably better than in most areas of Egypt, perhaps because of the long weaving tradition of the village and the high regard for clothing generally. Many kinds of fabrics are used and designs are area-specific and culturally meaningful. Each design has a name and all women know them. Styles change slightly over the life cycle of women and particular types of cloth and design are associated with life stages. The most popular and common French velvet gown or *galabeya* currently costs at least LE 30 (45 dollars), yet nearly all women own such a dress. Even *galabeyas* made from cotton or polyester have velvet yokes which are decorated. The simple headscarf and the formal visiting and mourning garment are also made by local female tailors.

This work is suitable for women who are confined to their homes with small children because they can work intermittently, can obtain all the materials locally, and because it depends only on local outlets. Women seldom have sufficient credit or income to purchase the expensive sewing machines necessary for tailoring and must therefore depend upon money or credit from their husbands. The Ministry of Social Affairs provides machines on easy terms to women who have completed sewing courses which they run, or women may borrow from the agricultural bank if husbands permit them and have sufficient credit to meet the bank's requirements. As in most cases, this work depends upon the goodwill of a husband or other male head of household.

Training for this work is managed through an unofficial system where older women teach the younger ones, who may or may not be related, in an apprentice system. If a young woman is interested she apprentices herself to a tailor and watches and assists with small tasks as she progresses. This is a very different and less

27

institutionalised form of apprenticeship from that generally practised in other crafts, where children are expected to work for parents, and women do not get paid while learning. It is one of the few occupations, however, which is considered suitable for women of all status groups.

Our three case studies in traditional crafts have very differing degrees of productive activity. Amina has married into a family which has been weaving for many generations. Safeya is part of a polygamous household which was formerly engaged in weaving and marketing cloth but which has changed to a more modern, related craft. Amal, on the other hand, did not come from or marry into a craft family, but has decided to become a tailor of women's *galabeyas* in order to earn cash, and she is very active in this work. Cases show the necessity of knowing family backgrounds as well as wider market and labour conditions before attempting to understand economic strategies of the household unit (see Appendix II).

Tourist crafts

Kerdassa is well known by Cairenes and other Middle Easterners for its tourist crafts. These include *galabeyas* of every description, mostly for women, tapestry weaving, locally known as *goblan,* and appliqué work. Prior to the last five years there were only two village merchants involved but gradually others began to flock to Kerdassa, especially from Gamalaya and the Khan el Khalili Bazaar in Cairo; at present, there are 51 shops in Kerdassa.

Merchants are becoming more vocal about problems, since the marketing capacity of the area seems to have been surpassed. In present conditions of increased competition, a number of things have happened to both the crafts and to the craftsmen producing for this market.

Firstly, quality has declined as merchants try to find the cheapest producer for a popular product. Oversupply has also driven prices down, and women especially have over-produced. Quality control has been enforced by merchants sporadically at best and mostly not at all, and price has been the determinant of what merchants will stock. This fall in quality has in turn affected sales.

Merchants who lacked marketing and management skills have found themselves increasingly poor, although some experienced merchants have been able to progress under present conditions. We found that some of the owners from the old bazaar area were people who had been producers there and who did not possess marketing or management skills. Both these newcomers and inexperienced village merchants find it difficult to compete against those bazaar merchants who have many years of experience selling to tourists and who come from families with a long tradition in the business.

The seasonal tourist cycle in Kerdassa follows European tourism in the winter and Arab tourism in the summer. The loss of Arab tourists in the past two years because of strained political relations has particularly affected the *galabeya* industry. Also, because of a scarcity of design skills, there has been a tendency for producers to copy each other's work. The cycle between introduction of a new style of *galabeya* or tapestry and total glut of the market is very short. Major merchants control design skills very closely and are forced to produce large amounts of new styles before releasing them on the market so that they can make a profit and then change to a new

28

design. This requires considerable capital outlay. Because small producers in both tapestry and *galabeyas* often lack skill and because there are no government or other training programmes, these producers are only able to copy the designs of others. They are lacking in ideas for original and innovative designs which will attract tourists. The paucity of culturally indigenous design ideas is evidenced in the fact that even Japanese and Chinese motifs are presently used in *galabeyas*.

The influx of outside merchants and products has affected the production of *galabeyas* and tapestries, in quite different ways.

Galabeyas

Production of *galabeyas* for the tourist trade was believed to be the largest source of employment for women in Kerdassa. The Family Planning Board has estimated that 1,500 women embroider *galabeyas* for this market in Kerdassa. In 1978 a colourful style of Bedouin *galabeya* inspired by Siwa oasis designs developed and has become a great favourite in the tourist trade. Women from the village made a good living from this embroidery which was organised as a cottage industry by merchants who supplied materials and paid women only for their labour. These merchants tried to control quality by not paying women for their work until *galabeyas* were sold, by refusing poor work, and by fining women the cost of the thread for products which were not of an acceptable quality. Very few people were able to produce the varied designs for this *galabeya* and they were mostly controlled by the major merchant in the village.

With the influx of city merchants came all the links which these shopowners had built up over the years in the urban bazaar. City producers not only copied the Siwa design and other Kerdassa styles, but they brought with them a great variety of new styles manufactured in small shops throughout the Cairo area. Women in Kerdassa could not compete with this influx of goods produced with better equipment and by male tailors with more experience and skill, and prices for the Siwa *galabeya* went down. As trade declined, the quality of work also declined, because women were less and less willing to spend large amounts of time sewing.

At the same time, the number of women who wanted to participate in embroidery grew because of a lack of alternatives for work that could be complementary to demanding social roles. This meant that women performing this one craft competed with each other and drove the price of their labour down. All these events coincided with a crisis in the world economy which caused a drop in tourist spending.

Currently, the market for embroidered *galabeyas* has declined, although some producers have managed to survive by expanding their markets to other areas, such as Khan el Khalili and Alexandria. One or two women have also been successful in organising other women and themselves becoming merchants.

Quite a large number of village tailors produce many other machine-finished styles which fill Kerdassan shops and which meet a growing demand. Most of these tailors have been connected with village merchants for a long time and some are very skillful, thus managing to compete. With the exception of three women who sew and decorate cheap cotton *galabeyas*, these tailors are men. Most work in shops in their own homes or in small rented workshops. The merchant supplies materials and pays the tailor for each *galabeya* produced. The quality of some of this work is very high and Egyptian city women are adopting these styles for home and even street wear.

Wives may assist these tailors by hand decoration such as beading, which is becoming increasingly popular, as are many kinds of elaborate machine decoration. A wide range of materials and designs cater to western, urban Egyptian, and Arab tastes. Prices range from LE 4 to LE 100, with cheaper *galabeyas* providing the largest and most dependable market. Because some small tailor shops own their own sewing machines, they are free to produce for any merchant. Kinship and supplier/client relationships may limit tailors' choices, however, and keep wages and thus expenses down for local merchants. Low wages, in turn, allow local merchants to claim a larger share of tourist business than city merchants.

Because they lack the training, management skills, access to credit and mobility, local women have not been able to enter into production of women's *galabeyas* which are machine-made and machine-decorated, although they dominate the manufacture of traditional women's wear.

Tapestry weaving

Tapestry weaving has existed in Egypt since Coptic times, when it was a highly developed art. It has not been practised locally for many years, but has gradually developed and was brought here from other areas of the Delta. In a neighbouring village a workshop was opened 20 years ago, and this subsequently became very famous for its artistic tapestries woven by children. Ramses Wissa Wassef, the founder of the school, has since died and his wife and daughters continue to run the school. Haraneya tapestries sell for extremely high prices to a sophisticated international fine art market and weavers trained in the school have been prevented from producing for private sale. For this reason, Haraneya has never generated important production in the area, although it has provided a reasonable living for a small number of local residents, many of whom are women. A second generation of weavers, often the children of the first generation, is now being trained in this school.

Haraneya served as a source of inspiration for the area and was greatly responsible for the revival of tapestry weaving. About eight years ago two Kerdassa merchants decided to begin selling tapestries and provided a few looms, bringing weavers from Sharkeya and Asyut to operate them. These cheap tapestries had a strong appeal to tourists from abroad as they depicted local flora and fauna and village scenes in a charming "primitive" style. Gradually Kerdassa weavers developed a number of themes and designs and began to improve the quality of the tapestries, which they called *goblan*. As other merchants flocked to the village they used their contacts to spread the production of *goblan* tapestries, which are now woven in many areas of Cairo and as far south as Asyut and which are sold in Khan el Khalili Bazaar.

Some of the more experienced and skilled weavers in Kerdassa attempt to copy directly from the designs of Haraneya. A few are producing good quality work but many poor products flood the market. Better weavers are beginning to sign their products and to think of themselves as artistic weavers. Only one, however, has taught his daughter to weave. As we show in a case study, wives of *goblan* weavers can be involved in production, if indirectly, and even though they do not receive cash for their activities.

Tapestry weavers work for particular merchants who supply them with wool and warping cotton. They are paid by production and depending upon the quality of each

30

piece, although they do not sometimes get paid until a piece is sold, despite their rates being higher than other weavers. As it takes many years to become a good weaver, most are using skills learned in other weaving occupations.

Some wool is purchased in the weekly market from women who handspin it, and then wash and dye it to suit individual weavers, but most wool is imported or bought from public sector mills. The market could easily be expanded for locally spun wool.

There is great variation in female participation in producing for the tourist trade, yet their production is low when compared with that of males. In the case studies, we compare the wife of a tailor producing machine-sewn and machine-trimmed *galabeyas* with the indirect participation of the wife of a tapestry weaver, and a woman embroidering *galabeyas*.

Subsistence crafts

We have chosen to term a certain number of handicrafts "subsistence crafts" because of their close association with household use. In the study, traditional handicrafts are those industries which have existed within the village for a long time but which are not quite as directly related to household function. This distinction is debatable in the cases of smithing or weaving, and is probably one of degree rather than kind.

Subsistence crafts present in Kerdassa include date palm industries, grass industry, basket making, and smithing. There is, as yet, insubstantial information about similar specialising villages in Egypt which exchange products with each other and which supply city markets, but a few others are known. Subsistence crafts might be defined by the small amount of capital involved in production and by low skill levels. These crafts thus provide work for many lower income families who do not have the necessary skills, education, or access to jobs in the more modern areas of the economy. All these crafts demand some training and depend upon skills transmitted within the household. They include producers of both sexes and more than one age group. Producers in this category often come from, or marry into, families which have specialised for three or more generations. Because of the loose organisation, they adapt readily to changes in market conditions and we note this in the case of the mat maker. The lack of written or precise oral history of these crafts prevents us from more effectively ascertaining changes which have occurred.

Date palm industries

Palm fibres have been extensively used for millenia in Egyptian culture, a fact attested to by the number of fragments discovered by archaeological expeditions. In the past, in fact, their use was probably far greater and more developed than it is today. In some areas, uses, styles, and methods of manufacture remain almost unchanged since the Ancient Dynastic Period. Kerdassa's location in the palm-rich Delta ensures an abundance of raw materials for these industries, which include *gereed*, palm stem products, *leef* or bark fibre industries.

Each year before the dates grow, farmers trim the outside leaves from palms, and these are then gathered and processed for related industries. The division of labour in this craft is very specialised and production is labour intensive. Leaves are purchased by the hundred for about LE 5 and brought, via donkey, to households which separate leaves from stems, and stack them for further distribution. The main stem is then sold to local producers of *gereed* or shipped to areas which lack palms. Leaves are sold for many types of basket and carrier, or to farmers for tying greens for market. During the remainder of the year leaf gatherers may be unemployed. One woman we talked to had taken over this heavy work after the death of her husband and she told us she was 60 or 70 years old. Judging from the age of her youngest child she could not have been more than 50, but her poverty and exhaustion had taken a toll not only on her body but also on her spirit. Many poor women are also employed making palm rope, fibre brooms, doormats and brushes for both urban and rural markets for pitifully small profits.

Palm leaves were used in ancient times for baskets, roofing, and wrapping. They are still used in Egypt for some of these purposes and have been adapted to modern markets in interesting ways, such as stuffing for modern furniture. The versatile *maktaf* basket also takes many forms and performs a myriad of functions which change through time. It is used in the household, in the fields and in the city.

Organisation for production is adjusted to a wide variation of family needs and structures. Producers' households are grouped and each specialises in producing and marketing a small range of products. An extended family may co-operate to run a small "factory" including an extensive cottage industry, and these larger producers have an advantage in their ability to adjust to difficult times. They can travel greater distances when materials are short and make a profit selling these to small producers, as they may own a truck or can rent one more easily. Cottage industries can contract or expand to meet current needs, as workers can be "laid off" at will. Large families with many young, strong males also have an advantage as they are more ambitious and flexible in marketing. Older producers and women usually sell their goods to larger merchants, asking little for their labour. The adaptabilities of this industry to the life cycle and structure of the family and low capital and skill requirements make it an excellent source of employment to meet temporary needs. Demand is constant, although producers are not guaranteed the sale of all products.

Palm leaf baskets are used in the wholesale and retail vegetable trade, for the transport of earth and food products by camel and donkey, for the export of dates, and the collection of refuse. In the Kerdassa weekly *suq*, leaf products occupy a considerable area. Local specialities are the very large, covered date basket, the commercial vegetable basket (*genba*), the two-handled carrying basket (*maktaf*), which comes in many sizes and qualities, and panniers for donkeys and camels (*hemla*). Marketing demands the availability of a cart and a donkey, which many families do not have.

There is a distinct sexual division of labour in *khoos* manufacture. Palm leaves are first dried, then soaked before working. They may be beaten to shreds for the manufacture of sewing twine, then hand-twisted. Unbeaten leaves are braided in a long strip which is then sewn from the inside with a large iron needle-like instrument. This sewing does not show from the outside and takes a considerable amount of strength to perform. The *zabila*, or flap is then made, or the basket is trimmed with fibre braid and handles may be attached. Women are concerned in all processes except sewing, which is always done by men. It is interesting that where females perform all functions except sewing they are never considered to be craftswomen, but are only believed to be "helping" male producers who are known as *khawass*.

32

The low skill levels necessary to perform the various functions in *maktaf* manufacture allow the use of a broad range of available family labour, and this is true in all subsistence crafts. It is also possible for some processes to be accomplished simultaneously with household duties such as watching children. Work can be picked up and put down at will and so is suitable for women occupied with young children or other family tasks. The breakdown of production into low skilled segments makes it suitable for old as well as young, and allows members of a family to replace each other. Technology levels are minimal.

Women do not sell *khoos* products, although they may sell both materials and products in all stages of manufacture in the *suq*. Educational levels in families involved in all palm industries are low for heads of household. However, there is a great variety of educational levels for children of producers. While many families do not send their children to school, others have made great sacrifices in order to see children, especially sons, stay at school. In families where children are at school, we found a large, active participation on the part of wives. We did not find females working in shops above the household level.

Grass industry (hasira)

Like the other subsistence crafts, *hasira* mats form part of household and religious customs. Mats identical to those manufactured today are found on archaeological sites from the Pharaonic period. These mats comprise one of the basic household furnishings for villagers and all mosques formerly covered their floors with these mats, a custom which is changing. Mats may have patterns woven in red or green and come in a range of sizes, or they may be made to order. Specially ordered mats are called *amoula* and are prized by villagers.

Large floor looms are needed for mat production and three mats are usually woven at one time. Because of the space necessary for the loom and because there is some level of skill necessary, this craft is less flexible than palm industries. *Samaar* reeds are not found in Kerdassa, so they must be purchased from other Delta areas or Fayum. A capital outlay is necessary for this industry. Only men weave mats, as it is strenuous and weavers work in teams of three, with a skilled weaver setting the pace and apprentices or less skilled labourers working on either side. Little preparation of materials is necessary except splitting off the blossoms from the grasses before use and daily stringing of the loom. Women or children assist in preparing food, feeding workers, and cleaning work areas.

Most production is household based, and four mat makers live in Kerdassa. Work is not seasonal and marketing takes place from the household or from the weekly *suq*. There is some urban demand but Kerdassa producers travel to surrounding village markets only. Workshops may employ workers or apprentices outside the family unit, and often do, partly because only male labour is used in manufacture. The industry is presently competing with machine-made and plastic imitations which are produced in more mechanised and larger workshops or imported. Although not as comfortable, plastic mats wear longer and wash more easily, and so are replacing natural grass mats.

Basket making

In addition to the *maktaf*, two other kinds of basket are produced in Kerdassa, the *sabbat* and the *mishana*. The *sabbat* is a stiff basket made from bamboo-like reeds *(gjab)* which grow in many areas of Egypt. The reed is first split with the teeth and a simple wooden tool is inserted and run down the reed to divide it into three sections. A two- or single-handled marketing basket is then woven from a circular base. Use is more limited than for the *maktaf* and we have noted only two sizes, one for daily marketing and one for transporting goods on the head. Women prepare reeds, manufacture these baskets and market them, travelling from rural to urban areas to sell them in the streets or selling directly to small shops in urban markets.

The *mishana* is a flat, round basket made of henna sticks which is widely used in the marketing of vegetables and in household storage. It comes in a variety of sizes and depths, mostly bowl-shaped. It is a strong basket, rather difficult to make because the sticks are stiff and scratch and chafe hands. Villagers say you can tell a basket maker when you shake hands because of his many callouses. Women and men make *mishana*, which are marketed in the village *suq* and in surrounding villages, but which are not in demand in urban markets.

Both henna and *ghab* must be transported by the truckload to Kerdassa from other Delta areas. Baskets require little skill, room, or strength to make and untrained and lower income families find this a good way to earn money. Production is grouped in one area where neighbours co-operate in obtaining materials and in marketing their production. Older children, mostly female, also contribute to production. Despite early denials, we found this work to be seasonal, with harvest periods being especially busy. Most people market their own production, unlike *maktaf*, and marketing is non-commercialised beyond the weekly *suq*, where women are prominent. Only family members are used as profits and capital are very low. A small number of families meet local needs.

Smithing

Both copper- and blacksmithing exist in Kerdassa, although in small numbers and serving only local needs. Changes are taking place in both these crafts which, because of the nature of the international metal trade, and because Egypt imports all metals, are more connected to world markets than other subsistence crafts. The role of copper production has decreased since the recent introduction of aluminium, despite its historic role as a dowry offering. In the study, we concentrate on the role of the traditional blacksmith (*hadad*) only.

The traditional *hadad* meets the household and farming needs of the community and for this reason has always held a special position in the community. It is the only craft in which myths exist.

Blacksmiths form a separate clan which intermarries to a much greater extent than the general population, and which, by tradition, does not attend school. The modern *hadad afrangi*, on the other hand, is an occupational category which requires training, usually in technical schools. These blacksmiths are literate and must make a considerable investment in modern equipment. They produce iron goods mostly for the building trades, fancy grillwork for gates, doors and windows, or stress-bars for concrete foundations. The *hadad afrangi* is usually young and operates from a workshop in a main street, in contrast to the traditional *hadad* who works from home with low technology levels, and using household labour, trained through a family apprenticeship system.

A very unusual fact about the traditional *hadad* is the use of female labour in the pounding of iron. Here women work alongside men, wielding heavy long-handled hammers in unison with them. We find this surprising in a country where men carry out the majority of productive tasks, even those usually occupied by women in other cultures and areas of the world.

The blacksmith builds a coal or coke fire outside his home and makes farm and household implements or repairs them with simple technology. His primary equipment is a fixed anvil (*sindal*) and a large stationery bellows (*koor*). Tools include the grasping tool (*talabat*), small hammer (*matra'a*) and the large hammer (*malzaba*). An iron tool *(mukash)* is used for stirring the fire. The major products of the traditional *hadad* are made from scrap iron which is either supplied by the customer or by the blacksmith, and include both basic household items and basic farm implements. These include: a stand for a water jar (*kursi zir*), a stand for a primus stove (*kursi babour*), the *mulokheya* knife or chopper (*makhrata*), a long tool for stirring the clay oven fire (*asa hadid*), the axe heads (*azma* and *balta*), and the hoe (*fas*). The large needle-like tool for *khoos* production is also manufactured by the *hadad*.

The *hadad* markets both from his home and in the weekly market, and may send women to travel to other villages selling goods. Women may also hawk goods in the streets. Because it is a skilled craft, a long apprenticeship is required and apprentices are recruited only from the family. To date the *hadad* is not an "endangered species" but limited technology and education prevent him from moving into the modern economy. His wages are much lower than those of the modern blacksmith who works in building trades. However, he still plays a vital role in the farming community and derives status from this.

The local myth that the *hadad* was once very rich but that in the heat of a family quarrel between brothers one brother threw all their money into the fire, and so now they are relatively poor may have its origin in the competition between brothers that we witnessed in every small industry. It may also be an attempt to explain the current low income in comparison with the more modern occupation. We notice in our case study the high incidence of endogamous marriage in two related extended (polygamous) families, the change in attitude towards education, and the severing of family members into other occupations, although this is as yet unexplained.

Notes
1) These figures were supplied by the Family Planning Board. We are unclear as to the meaning of the term "family" as used by the Board, as this term is imprecise.

IV. CASE ANALYSIS: PRODUCTIVE AND REPRODUCTIVE ROLES

The eleven women

We attempt here to analyse attitudes, beliefs, and concepts of certain women in Kerdassa in their roles as mothers, wives, workers inside and outside the home, and kin. The basic life circumstances of the case studies are reviewed in table 1. Case descriptions will be found in Appendix II (p. 59).

All women chosen for the case studies are Moslem. Three are between 20 and 24, four between 25 and 29, one between 30 and 34, and three are between 35 and 40 years. All are married and of childbearing age. All are illiterate except one, who has a secondary school education (Jihan). Four women married between the ages of 11 and 15, six married between 16 and 20, and one married at age 30. Four women live in nuclear households, two live in polygamous households, three live in extended families, and two reside in nuclear units located in family compounds. None lives in a joint household. Eight of the families own no land, two have between 0 and 1 *feddan*, and one has over 5 *feddans*. Five women have running water at home and six must carry water for family use. Five raise chickens or animals for family use and food, another raises animals for sale, and four raise no animals or chickens. The brideprice (*mahr*) paid for women in the cases ranges from LE 0–50 (3), LE 50–100 (3), LE 110–500 (2), to over LE 1000 (1); two are unreported on this issue. *Mahr* cannot be used as a status symbol on this small scale but is related to years married and change in brideprice over time. The cases were chosen to illustrate particular points of importance. (See case studies in appendix for difference in family types.)

Household production and children

Participation in non-agrarian production (exclusive of subsistence activities) varies across the sample from light to very heavy. The case descriptions speak for themselves on this issue and we hope they will broaden current definitions of women's work. As Hoda Fahmy's research showed, women were inclined to classify their participation in three different categories:

Category 1 – **Socially obligatory work**

When a woman helps her husband in his craft, this is not considered an end in itself, but is connected to her sex and social roles. She sees it as an obligation or a duty and she often expresses her attitude to it as "exhausting work" or "tiring work". She sees herself as a "helper", not a producer, and is referred to as this by others.

Category 2 – **Voluntary work**

When a husband has a fixed occupation and income, as an employee in a governmental agency, for example, even if he

TABLE 1

LIFE CIRCUMSTANCES OF THE ELEVEN WOMEN

NAMES	OCCUPATION	PRODUCTIVE ROLE (1)			HUSBAND'S OCCUPATION	EDUCATION	HUSBAND'S EDUCATION	RESIDENCE PATTERN	NUMBER IN HOUSEHOLD
		a	b	c					
AMINA	BEADING GALABEYAS	X			FACTORY WORKER	NONE	NONE	EXTENDED	6
SAFEYA	VERSALIA MAKER			X	VERSALIA MERCHANT	NONE	NONE	POLY-GAMOUS	10
AMAL	TAILOR			X	MECHANIC	NONE	–	NUCLEAR-FC(4)	6
HALIMA	EMBROIDERING GALABEYAS	X			STOCKIST FOR LOCAL MERCHANT	NONE	5 YRS	NUCLEAR	5
NAGUA	EMBROIDERING GALABEYAS		X		MECHANIC/ GALABEYA MERCHANT	NONE	8 YRS	NUCLEAR	7
JIHAN	TAILOR		X		TAILOR	12 YRS	12 YRS	NUCLEAR-FC(4)	3
SAMIRA	NONE		X		TAPESTRY WEAVER	NONE	8 YRS	NUCLEAR	10
NASARA	NONE		X		MAT MAKER	NONE	NONE	EXTENDED	6
MARYAM	BASKET MAKER			X	BASKET MAKER	NONE	NONE	NUCLEAR	8
NAFISA	BASKET MAKER		X		BASKET MAKER	NONE	NONE	EXTENDED	8
HAMIDA	BLACK-SMITH			X	BLACK-SMITH	NONE	NONE	POLY-GAMOUS	8
TOTALS									

38

Table — household/reproductive data (CONTROL OVER spans the columns OWN LABOUR, OTHERS LABOUR, INCOME FROM LABOUR, REPRODUCTIVE CAPACITY, OTHER RESOURCES)

LAND	ANIMALS	ELECTRICITY	WATER	OVEN	TV	AGE	AGE AT MARRIAGE	YEARS MARRIED	PREGNANCIES	LIVE BIRTHS	SPONTANEOUS ABORTIONS	CHILD DEATHS	SURVIVING CHILDREN	SONS	DAUGHTERS	CHILDREN IN SCHOOL	USE OF PUBLIC HEALTH CLINIC	PRE-NATAL CARE	POST-NATAL CARE	EVER CONTRACEPTIVE USE	DELIVERY BY DAYA	OWN LABOUR	OTHERS LABOUR	INCOME FROM LABOUR	REPRODUCTIVE CAPACITY	OTHER RESOURCES	BRIDEPRICE (LE) (3)
		X				24	20	4	2	2	0	0	2		2		X	X			X		X				–
1K (7)	X	X				35	20	15	14	8	6	2	6	3	3	2					Ab (2)	X		X (9)			40
		X	X	X	X	27	19	8	2	2	0	0	2	1	1	1	X		X		X		X				–
		X		X		28	17	11	9	6	3	3	3	2	1	2		X	X		Ab (2)	X				X	100
		X				27	14	13	5	5	0	0	5	1	4	3		X			X						200
8F (8)	X	X	X	X	X	21	18	3	2 (5)	1	0	0	1		1						X	X	X		X	X	1300
		X	X	X		25	20	5	3	3	0	0	3		3		X	X	X		X						100
		X		X		23	13	10	7	5	2	2	3	1	2	2					Ab (2)	X					150
		X	X		X	34	12	22	15	13	2	7	6	3	3	2			X	X	Ab (2)				X (10)		40
11K (7)	X	X	X	X	X	39	11	28	12	12	0	7	5	1	4	2	X	X	X	X	X			X (10)	X	X	70
	X	X				40	30	10	3	5 (6)	0	4	1		1			X			X						30
3	4	11	5	6	4				74	62	13	25		13	24	14	4	6	5	2	11	4	3	2	3	3	

Notes:

1. Non-agricultural (non-subsistence) activities: a = light; b = medium; c = heavy
2. Ab = spontaneous abortion haemorrhage only
3. LE = $ 1.50
4. Nuclear-FC = nuclear unit within compound
5. Pregnant
6. Two double pregnancies
7. K = Kirat
8. F = Feddan = 1.04 acres
9. Son
10. Daughter

works in a craft industry as well, a woman feels more free to participate or not, and if she does she expresses much less fatigue, even though she does not get paid.

Category 3 – "Real" work

If a woman is involved in a productive activity on her own and she is the main entrepreneur, this is felt by her to be self-fulfilment. Only then does she use the Arabic term "work" (*shugl*) referring to her distinct role as a producer.

Seven women in the study experienced no sense of esteem or personal gratification from productive work done separately from household chores and childcare. Of the four who did, all controlled their earnings, while only one in the former category did so. This latter case (Nafisa) performs work which she feels is beneath her family status, and this may explain the fact that although she controls money she gains no sense of reward from her work. Some women who had no choice about the work they did nevertheless felt that either their husbands or others saw them as more competent because they could perform tasks, solve problems, or earn money. Pleasing their husbands was a source of pleasure even to women who found no satisfaction in work.

Three women who had no control over money earned expressed a desire to do so and three thought this was unimportant. Where women thought they should control their earnings but did not, there seemed to be a conflict between spouses. Where women handled income but did not consider this important (Halima, Nafisa), there was no discernible conflict, perhaps because spouses agreed on this issue.

Only three women in the study had any choice about the kind of work they did (Amal, Jihan, Halima). Others were expected to assist husbands whether they desired to or not. Half of the cases desired to work in income-producing employment and half had no desire to do so. Of the first half, three were employed in household production for which they were not paid. Two were currently unemployed. Only one was fulfilling her desire. Of those who did not desire cash-producing employment, all were employed in household crafts out of necessity, and only one controlled any household income.

Two women were paid for their labour and both controlled the use of their income (Amal, Halima). Two were unpaid but controlled family resources (Jihan, Nafisa). A fifth moved from unpaid work to controlling family resources when her husband died (Safeya). Six were unpaid and had no direct control over family income despite high labour inputs.

The deepest conflicts were noted in households where spouses disagreed about decision-making power over resources. The women's major source of complaint was related to very individual life circumstances, although women expressed discontent with marriage to husbands in low status work whether they came from low status families or not.

Women who were the least inclined to justify themselves in moralistic terms, that is, to stress their superior moral qualities in comparison with others, were those controlling most resources. Women who had experienced many child deaths and who controlled no resources were most likely to express themselves in moral or religious terms (Safeya is an exception to this). All cases were Muslim women and their religious commitment varied throughout the sample. Few expressed any awareness of wider economic or social conditions, but where this did occur it was related to family status, education, access to political power, wealth and urbanisation.

Four women preferred extended or polygamous family residence to nuclear residence. One of these preferred living in a nuclear unit, separate from in-laws, yet wanted her son to remain in her household after marriage. This is not surprising given the difference in decision-making power and household status between young, subordinate wives and mothers-in-law. This informant was young and held a tenuous position in the extended family. Two other women expressed a desire for nuclear residence and both had realised this desire. Female work groups are organised within the extended family, as is assistance and support in times of illness or crisis. Many women, we believe, are reluctant to give up this support.

Only two women felt it was unnecessary to educate their daughters. Three others had some reservations, believing that lower levels of education (primary or preparatory levels) were sufficient for them. Women who expressed a need for the labour of their daughters placed a low value on female education. Most women in the study saw education as the key to new and better jobs, personal development, increased marriage choices, or simply higher status for their daughters. Most of the women, however, believed education was more important for their sons than for their daughters.

It is evident that even where patriarchal norms prevail, women are expected to provide for themselves and their children when husbands are unable to do this adequately. Women are also expected to bear large numbers of children, to assist their husbands in household industries, to prepare and serve food and in many instances to provide this food even after their children have married and set up households of their own. Women are expected to do this with technological assistance which has changed little over thousands of years, although technology in other sectors of the economy and in male-dominated activities has been upgraded. They also contribute to this labour and reproductive capacity with little or no pre- or post-natal care and with a diet insufficient for female needs.

Fertility and family planning

In household production there was a positive correlation between childbearing and labour force participation. We find an average of 8.3 pregnancies for women with heavy productive roles, as against 2.3 for women with weak productive roles, and 6.72 average over the sample as a whole.[1]

There are certain problems in attempting to compare fertility statistics for this group by age, the primary one being the small number sampled. Secondly, the fact that two of the 11 women are members of polygamous households and, in both instances, second wives who married late, makes the sample unreliable. Only one observation is evident from comparing live births and duration of marriage against age, and that is that the reproduction of the women in five-year spans remains quite remarkably constant over a 30-year period. Women continue to bear children at a somewhat constant rate throughout their married life and this rate is only slightly lower at both ends of the time span.

There were 74 pregnancies reported overall and 37 of these survived. We also find the highest number of spontaneous abortions and child deaths among more

41

economically active women. Among strongly productive women we find nearly 2 spontaneous abortions on average and 3.3 child deaths, as against the whole sample averages of 1.2 and 2.3. Women in this sample who were not heavily involved in production or assisting husbands experienced no spontaneous abortions or child deaths. This is not necessarily related to work but more probably to preferred family status of these women, their youth, better diet and health care.

The number of infant deaths in our sample is staggeringly high. Two women experienced seven losses each (both very productive women). There were 25 child deaths out of a total of 74 pregnancies and 62 live births (two double births). Many of these babies died in the first week (11), nine more died within the first month, and an additional three died within a year. Two children died between one and five years. Thirteen spontaneous abortions were reported and 37 children survive. In other words, half of the children conceived survived to the age of five and 59 per cent of live births survived to the age of 3. The cost of this wastage to the lives and strength of rural women is appallingly high. We would like to stress the fact that Kerdassa is only 15 kilometres from Cairo and only 10 kilometres from central Giza. Effective ways must be found to decrease this wastage in female and child life. In the study we also find that fear of child death influences attitudes of women toward pregnancy, increasing pro-natal attitudes.

Half of the women stated that they needed children to care for them in their old age. Only two thought daughters might help and all five expected sons to help them. This suggests that women may attempt to provide enough sons to be sure at least one survives to help them when they become older or if their husbands should die.

Other reasons which women gave for desiring children were:

to reinforce their position in the extended family (power over decision-making, over labour of others);

enjoyment of children;

children were a gift of God;

the need for a son;[2]

the need for child labour. Conversely, a woman engaged in work where children are not employed desires fewer children;

to gain self-esteem. Fulfilment of social expectations brings higher community status;

pleasing a husband;

religious belief that it is against the will of God to limit births;

belief that they are not in control of their productive capacity. This is related to their control over other resources and to general decision-making power.[3]

Women were divided (six to five) in their desire for large numbers of children. Women who expressed a desire for large families had many pregnancies and those who sought to limit the number of their children did not, except for Hamida who would have preferred to have more surviving children than she had. The three women who experienced repeated child deaths desired many children.

42

Only five women had ever used the public health unit. Among those who used it, evaluations ranged from "better than nothing" to "useless". Some attended the clinic for one or two pregnancies then stopped. Several felt that the quality of care had decreased in the clinic. Several had never been visited by nurses or family planning workers. Some complained about the inconsistent supply of certain brands of contraceptive pills. One case (Samira) gave different answers to two researchers and her results are uncertain. Seven women used private medical care in case of illness, especially if serious. Three could not afford it and usually did without medical care. Two used the public health units in case of illness or emergency.

All women used the *daya* for deliveries, except one who gave contradictory opinions. One other woman had a doctor called in when her delivery proved difficult (Jihan). Both women using doctors in addition to *dayas* were either of higher status or of urban origin. Five other women had been to hospitals for spontaneous abortions which had resulted in haemorrhage. None confessed to attempted abortion, although we know from local doctors and hospitals that women are admitted in late stages of septicaemia from abortions attempted at home, and some women subsequently die. If they die, the persons responsible are sought and interrogated, a practice which makes women reluctant to seek competent medical advice in cases of infection from attempted abortion. Aside from hospital treatment for haemorrhage, no pre- or post-natal care was given to the women apart from Jihan, who received check-ups for a second pregnancy, after difficulties in the first delivery.

Only two women had ever used contraceptive methods and both of these had spaced births using contraceptive pills. All knew about pills and some other contraceptive methods, yet most were ill informed as to actual differences or effects. Many preferred to believe local female gossip accentuating negative aspects or effects which often could not be caused by these methods. Attitudes to contraception improved in the one case where the woman was educated. Several women expressed a wish to use pills to prevent births when they had attained the desired number of children. One woman has become pregnant recently while supposedly taking birth control pills (Samira).

Five women felt that they could decide for themselves whether to limit births, five believed their husbands should decide and two believed it was up to God and their husbands. One other thought God should decide. Only one decided with her husband (Nafisa) and two made no decisions at all. Both women in higher status families thought they could decide (Amal, Jihan). Nasara is an interesting case as she exhibits an instance where changing family circumstances brought about an abrupt change in attitudes toward pregnancy, which may or may not actually be implemented. Nasara's husband has told her that they should not have any more children, but positive measures to limit births have not yet been taken. Poor health in women was not usually a factor in deciding to limit births. Of the five women who thought they could decide to limit their fertility, only two had actually done so, both against the wishes of their husbands (Samira, Amal).

Five women expressed a belief that breast feeding prevents pregnancy. We are concerned that in one case of bottle feeding there may be a connection between this and the extremely high rate of infant mortality. This is due perhaps to contamination through poor hygiene practices in washing and handling bottles and in transporting water. One woman became pregnant when she believed she could not because she was breast feeding and another does not want more children but is not taking any

43

precautionary measures because of her belief that breast feeding protects her, as it has in the past.

Three women expressed a preference for boys and two of these said it was because sons inherit and daughters do not. This is an important point, stressing differences between actual practice and Muslim family law (*shari'a*) which governs inheritance, and should be further researched. The case of Maryam shows that where few brothers exist a woman may inherit more easily.

All deliveries were at home except for Hamida, who was taken to hospital after losing four infants soon after birth. Half (five) of the women went to the home of their mother for delivery and a sixth had her mother present in her home. One woman (Maryam) had no female relatives available to assist her at birth. Four women expressed fears about child survival and all of these had experienced child deaths.

From the case studies presented, it would appear that there is a relationship between a highly productive role and high reproduction in the cases where the women are actively involved in their husband's craft and therefore indispensable to them. While their actual number of living children may be only slightly above average, for these women the number of pregnancies is extremely high.

One explanation for bearing children given by the women is that they need additional labour to increase their productivity and they cannot afford to pay for expensive wage labour. The attitudes of the women studied also show that poor families who are involved in a craft and who live from day to day are unable to plan their lives and are more likely to believe that everything is in God's hands.

We notice that most of the women in the study are financially dependent upon their husbands, despite their productive life, and are unpaid if they work for their husbands. Husbands in most cases are decision-makers in family planning and other matters, and therefore, even where wives feel exhausted from many pregnancies or desire to limit births, they may feel obliged to comply with their husband's wishes and are often reluctant to express opposing opinions. This is most evident in those cases where women are totally dependent, and it is unrelated to the degree of their participation in production. In contrast, we find women who are very active in productive life but not financially dependent upon husbands. Here attitudes towards family planning are not the decision of the husband. Individual life circumstances and family status influence this more than labour input.

The striking thing in all cases is the importance of the *daya* in Kerdassa. All women in the study, including those with education and those from prestigious families, favour the *daya* and prefer to have her in attendance rather than a doctor. The four *dayas* in the village have gained the sympathy and trust of the women as they live among them and are able to communicate with them and understand their needs and desires. Women also prefer to deliver either in their own homes or the homes of their mothers.

In times of serious illness women prefer to go to a public hospital in Cairo rather than to the local public clinic and do so if they cannot afford a private physician. The public clinic, as shown in all the case studies, has failed to fulfil its role. Women who register at the clinic become discouraged when they find it offers nothing, and in subsequent pregnancies do not even bother to register. This is true in spite of the high number of infant deaths and frequent spontaneous abortions. Many women have said that the public clinic was better in the past in terms of services offered. At present, neither medicines nor consultations are given, despite government pressures to implement family planning. Women are also reported as being unable to buy constant supplies of some types of pill and so are forced to change constantly. Even worse, they are often unable to afford contraceptive devices which are available and so become discouraged. They may pay for more expensive types which are available, or they may stop using any contraceptive device at all. These problems of implementation of desire to limit families need to be addressed at the national and local levels.

Most women have heard of the pill and the loop, and one or two have heard about the condom. Most have reported bad health effects based upon false rumours, which are propagated from neighbour to neighbour because of the lack of any education about real results and effects. No serious effort is being made to spread awareness among women who are at present completely ignorant of these devices. Even if women want to use contraceptive devices they may be worried by rumours and so continue to bear unwanted children, believing that contraceptive devices may cause more harm than repeated pregnancies.

Families who have experienced repeated child deaths either through sickness or accidents are the most reticent about contraceptive devices. These women express a strong religious attitude as illustrated in the cases presented. While no woman listed fear of child death among the reasons for having children, we found in the studies that it is prevalent.

Women's status

At the community level, status is related to wealth, land, material possessions, occupation, access to power, and to family position and reputation. There is an increasing difference between groups within the village, brought about by accumulation of wealth in certain families and reinforced by increasingly centralised power structures and through increased access of upper status families to markets, and to education and training, and thus, new job opportunities in the modern economic structure.

Although some status remains in families of particular traditional craftsmen, such as weavers, this is dwindling because of their increasing impoverishment. Other crafts have had low status for some time, especially those requiring less skill, as culturally defined, and shorter training periods.

Women's status is not dependent upon labour input, rather the reverse is true in household production where input is related to the husband's work. Low social status in some crafts affects those families who participate in this work, so only women from low status families labour in these crafts. Women's status is generally related to that of their families, and family status affects their exercise of certain powers vis-à-vis husbands, such as decision-making, distribution of resources, control over their fertility, and the work they will do. However, women can increase their status in the community, and that of their children, through higher education or work opportunities which bring them income they can use to educate, feed, and clothe children. Higher education has its own status and brings increased dowry and marriage choices. Both education and income improve women's power vis-à-vis husbands to implement choices in distribution and control of resources, including their labour and fertility. As education is a function of family status it is *only* through income-generating work that women of lower status can hope to break out of the presently existing status-reinforcing cycle.

45

Evidence of change

There is evidence in Kerdassa of changes which are affecting women. The movement of men into wage labour should be viewed for its effects on women (see cases of Amal and Amina). These changes are not the same for women in all groups. Where males are paid at piecework rates, we also see how this work has included the unpaid participation of women and has thrown added expense and responsibility upon the household (see cases of Jihan, Samira, Nagua).

Cross-generational changes generally witness the lower participation of women in productive labour where men work for wages, or where they move to related crafts (see Nasara's case). Unpaid female labour may be increased, however, in some instances (as with Safeya). Women are more dependent upon males economically where husbands have entered the paid labour force and where women no longer produce as paid or unpaid workers.

The cultural value for non-productive women is firmly established in Kerdassa and has been adopted at all status levels. However, we see a change in this value where women need to work because of pressures caused by inflation. Attitudes have changed where some women wish to work, and these are also seen in raised hopes that children, especially girls, will be educated and will work for wages. Different rates of attitudinal change exist, however, and expectations have not changed in some cases (Maryam). Other women may make the conservative choice of withdrawing into the household rather than use education and status to assist in community and female development (Jihan).

There has been a rise in age at marriage which is expected to affect the fertility statistics of those now marrying.

The demise of traditional crafts has affected the skill structure and usefulness of these skills. The apprentice system in the past focused upon a sexual division of labour which is now changing and which favours males in current changes for skill demands. Women need help to overcome this inequality.

Although we often find increased motivation and raised aspirations regarding both work participation and family planning, there are indications that health services have decreased over time. This affects the implementation of desires in both production and family planning on the individual level, and slows government aims in these areas as well. The ability for low income women, especially, to implement desires, has been affected by this decrease in services.

Women's needs

Planners need to examine the failure of the family planning programme to reach lower income women. This seems partly due to a misunderstanding about the way in which things in the village are accomplished and a lack of recognition of differential access to communication channels, decision-making and resources. In reassessment of work already carried out by the Family Planning Board, it would be helpful to look more carefully at the categories of women's participation in production. The nature of relations within the household must be investigated further to determine decision-making patterns in rural areas and how variations in these patterns are associated with work patterns, status groups, and fertility levels.

Better basic health care for lower income women is essential in lowering infant death rates and female mortality, and in raising health standards. Family planning motivation cannot be separated from health conditions or from expectations for child survival. Training programmes to familiarise local, traditional *dayas* with sanitation practices and basic health precautions could go a long way in assisting both health and family planning aims, as these *dayas* serve women in many capacities already throughout their lives and have gained their trust and confidence. Programmes of this sort are meeting with success in other areas of the Middle East, such as the Yemen Arab Republic, and were known in Egypt under Nasser. We suggest the introduction of this training. *Hakimas*, or nurse-midwives, who have been trained in Western ideas regarding nursing or midwifery which do not take into account local traditions and beliefs surrounding childbirth, may be considered outsiders by village women.

Education for rural women needs to take into consideration current economic and labour conditions and real income needs. Programmes are necessary for adult women who are currently uneducated to gain skills and find employment. Firm social commitment and direction of resources are needed to achieve this end. Employment should be realistically designed to minimise the impact on current social structures so that women may not feel pressure from inability to meet social demands. Small, local programmes, income-generating schemes, and co-operatives could employ local women in joint training and production programmes.

Notes

1) We recognise the statistical insignificance of a sample this size and offer these figures for comparative purposes only.
2) Women may continue bearing children until one or more sons is produced. They also stated "sons inherit, daughters don't".
3) Reasons are not listed in order of priority.

V. CONCLUSION

Summary of findings

As we have shown, women contribute much to the subsistence economy and handicraft production in Kerdassa. We have noted certain trends which are occurring and which will affect the status of women. Most important, women are not moving into the modern forms of production in the capitalising economy but are remaining in increasingly unrewarding forms of labour. Although their labour input remains constant, they receive little reward for this labour and because technological advances bypass areas of production where women participate, they are unable to compete with men. Women are also crowding into the few areas of production where lack of education, skills, or mobility are unimportant, thus driving the price of their labour down as they compete with each other. We have noted a shift in the sexual division of labour in favour of men, who now perform tasks which formerly were considered only women's work, such as production of women's clothing or chicken farming. As areas of production become capitalised, women's lack of access to capital and credit and lack of mobility prohibit them from retaining control over these tasks. The long-term result will be a decrease in the status of women vis-à-vis men as they control fewer and fewer resources.

Rural areas may resist capitalisation because of female inputs, thus resulting in stability of subsistence economy. Women's contributions also keep wages down in other sectors of the economy and allow growth which would not otherwise be possible. This resistance to commoditisation may occur because of:

1) the contribution of women to the household and subsistence economies. If male wage earners employed in or outside the village are temporarily out of work, the household can subsist through increasing efforts, lowering consumption, and partially withdrawing from market relations (Shanin, 1972). The women's contribution allows merchants and employers in all areas to pay lower wages. In cottage production many production costs are pushed onto households, thus allowing merchant profits to be higher.

2) locally circulating markets in certain basic commodities are not directly connected to outside markets. This enables women to buy and sell at prices based on personal relationships as well as on wider market prices. Women may also obtain credit this way. Basic subsistence commodities circulating in this manner are grain (wheat and corn), cheese, fowl, greens and legumes.

In order to support these predictions precise data might be collected on household expenditures in both local and other markets. Expenditures should be compared between households where females participate in subsistence activities, in agriculture, in crafts, and in other occupations. To date evidence is not available in a form which is complete enough for this purpose.

Inflationary pressures are exaggerated on households of small producers where wages and prices of goods they produce are standardised and rise more slowly than prices for purchased goods. Women in these households are badly in need of cash and work long hours for small returns in order to survive. However, there is some relationship between household size and labour productivity, accumulation, and marketing advantage. Households with large numbers of males may have an advantage, yet poorer families are able to use surplus female labour to increase income. Subsistence levels depend largely upon the number of productive members and this changes over the life cycle of the family. Younger families with large numbers of unproductive children may be at a distinct disadvantage, especially in those groups which lack education and skills.

Women in different status groups had access to different occupations. Family status determined ability to choose work, labour input, and chances of getting paid for work or controlling money earned from work. The labour of women who assisted their husbands was not socially recognised or labelled, either by them or by others. Where women were able to choose work, relationships with husbands were affected; they had more decision-making power over distribution of income and over choices in general. These women were also able to implement their desires in the matter of childbearing. Relationships within the household affected fertility patterns of these women, increasing live births, child survival, fertility control, and decreasing wastage. Where women could not choose work or did not have decision-making power over resources, they did not believe they could control fertility.

Fertility levels had a positive correlation with labour input in household industries, and especially in those in which child labour was useful to women. Where women chose work and controlled income from work and where this work did not use child labour, women attempted to limit fertility. Women who had not chosen their work but who performed socially obligatory productive roles in household industries, did not see this labour as a way for themselves or their children to gain social status or improved conditions. These women wanted their sons to be educated and not to follow in the steps of their family, preferring that they take government posts or work in jobs with stable salaries. Some women saw education as a route open to social benefits for daughters, although others did not see this, believing that daughters would marry young and labour in the way they did. Women who saw no hope of improvement were not inclined to limit their fertility.

Only one woman in the case studies had any education. Government training programmes designed to assist women in finding income-generating work in Kerdassa had failed to relate to women's real needs or to current demands for skills. Attempts to provide health care and family planning information had also failed to reach lower income groups in the village. Women in higher status groups had access both to communication channels on health care and family planning and to better care. This resulted in higher fertility levels in the most needy group and in higher levels of infant mortality, which also affected women's attitudes to bearing children — women who had experienced repeated child deaths bore, or wished to bear, many children. While women did use public services in the event of delivery difficulties or dangerous haemorrhaging, they preferred urban hospitals to local facilities. All women in the study preferred *dayas* to deliver their children over either nurse-*hakimas* or physicians.

Most women wanted many children for a variety of reasons, most commonly to have sons, to provide security for old age, to help with work, or to gain approval of husbands. Even where women wished to limit births because they already had enough children, because of work and expense in raising them, because of failing health, or because they did not need them for labour, they had difficulty carrying out their desires. This was due primarily to lack of decision-making power (husband decided), fatalism and fear of the effects of contraceptives. Where women knew nothing about contraceptives and real effects and differences, they believed negative rumours passed on by other women.

Policy implications

From observations in other areas of Egypt we know that no generalisations can be made to cover all villages. Village and area autonomy are both marked and use of female labour differs greatly. We have seen a general trend, however, substantiated in Kerdassa, for women to move out of household production when family businesses become lucrative enough so that substitutes may be employed. There are, however, too few areas of production into which they can at present move. As women are not organised beyond the extended family in Egypt, we believe these two restraints on the expansion of craft industries provide a challenge to planners who are proposing income-generating schemes for women. Women who are household heads (widows and divorced, or single women) do not have the option of leaving work and may thus provide a focus for the planned inclusion of female labour. Pilot projects should be attempted, using these women as organisers and foci. The stiff competition between brothers in household industry is also noted. This major point, in a primarily kinship-organised productive system, also inhibits expansion of handicrafts. A fourth consideration in planning for the inclusion of handicrafts into the wider economic system is the fact that handicrafts seldom generate enough capital for accumulation and expansion, and so these funds must come from other areas. At present many women are employed by rich men who have a monopoly control over the market. One possible way of improving their position is the organisation of producers' co-operatives for the production of traditional and tourist-aimed handicrafts.

Another vital implication of the study in regard to work is the understanding it provides of the lack of provision of meaningful training schemes for women. We can see here how lack of understanding of real needs of rural women can result in wasted time, effort, and resources. Thus, for example, sewing courses prepared by government agencies have not trained women to do work which could provide a substantial income for them and for their families. A more sophisticated view of demand and regional co-ordination needs to be studied by vocational training experts in Egypt, and a firm social commitment must be made and supported, to provide rural women with education, skills and projects, which will enable them to fulfil their real potential in contributing to economic development. Failure to exploit available human resources to date has increased pressures on single wage-earner families and has slowed both industrial development and the improvement of social welfare for lower income groups. As we see in the study, it also affects fertility rates.

In the move from subsistence and traditional crafts to tourist crafts, which are largely organised and dominated by males, the women's contribution in handicrafts decreases. This trend began long ago, however, in some traditional crafts such as

51

weaving, which have moved into workshops outside the household. In this move, male labour is substituted for tasks formerly done by females (spinning, dyeing, bobbin winding, for example). Women have a doubtful monopoly only in the production of women's clothing, where males control cloth distribution, thread, trim, and beading. We show the resourceful use of female labour in *versalia,* a craft which is derived from weaving, where traditional skills have been used as a basis for a new industry, linked to modern ready-made clothing and luggage production. This is a rare example of how the development of work for women in the modern economy is possible, although lack of education, skills, credit, capital and access to modern technology have generally eliminated them.

Despite the decreased viability of crafts which compete directly with machine production, such as weaving, we see continued vitality in crafts with a strong cultural significance and those which are produced from local raw materials. By developing markets for these products and assisting in distribution, government planners could expand this type of work for women.

The dependence on female labour in the subsistence economy for production, processing, and preparation of food, and for washing, cleaning, serving, producing and rearing children has remained constant or may even have increased due to inflation and male migration. There is increasing class differentiation as women move from production to consumption and become reproducers of the labour force only. As dependence of females on males is valued in a patriarchal society, this value is realised by those able to do so (see Jihan's case).

The study has attempted to deal with the question of women's productive role not only as it relates to narrow Western definitions of work, but in the wider context of women's contribution to society as a whole. We believe it is only in this way that we can relate the status of women vis-à-vis men to social reality. We hope that once we have defined women's contributions and their conditions of struggle, both national policies and private opinions which seek to conceal and distort this contribution may be enlightened. It is only then that we can hope for the introduction of new policies which include women on an equal footing with men, so that all members of society may benefit from this contribution.

Conditions of poverty are exacerbated where women are unable to earn income to meet the increasing costs of food and education. Lower income and status groups may also fail to realise their aims to limit family size or may not want to do so, because they see children as a realisable resource to gain future security and assistance otherwise denied them. Alternatively, they may see themselves as simply unable to control fertility as they are unable to control or fulfil other aspirations. In these conditions general family welfare declines.

Two factors are especially important in blocking these groups from improving their lifestyle:

a) The paternalistic social structure which denies women mobility, credit, or autonomy and which subordinates them to males whose aims do not necessarily coincide with those of females within the household;

b) Government policies, which fail to assess adequately female needs in employment, co-operative formation, education, or training programmes, or in basic health care and effective fertility programmes. Although local health clinics do exist they are not assisting this section of the population to understand family planning, basic health methods, and sanitation improvement.

The decision of policy-makers to increase work opportunities through support for co-operative formation, education and skill training which considers the needs of women will result in raised real incomes, increased autonomy and decision-making influence, and decreased fertility. The dedication of government to eradicating the impediments to this group's realisation of these goals can be done at little increased cost by re-evaluation and adjustment of current aims in both health care and vocational training. This can be started by refocusing statistical analyses to better conceived productive categories within lower status and income groups in rural areas, and by attempting to understand the dynamics of work atmosphere, type, level and fertility behaviour, including both desire for children and ability to implement desire.

We offer this study as a contribution to such an endeavour.

APPENDIX I

Methods of fieldwork

General method

The project was a collaborative effort by Patricia D. Lynch, an American anthropologist and Ph.D. candidate in social anthropology at the University of Cambridge, England, and Hoda Fahmy, an Egyptian anthropologist possessing an M.A. in anthropology from the American University in Cairo and having considerable field and project experience, under the auspices of the Egyptian Center for Civilization Studies, Cairo. The project took place from August 1980 to June 1981, with Lynch spending five days per week in the village from October 1980 to January 1981, and making shorter trips during the remainder of the year. Fahmy had a previous one year period of residence in the village and, whilst carrying out her research in March and April 1981, she made day trips there.

The initial survey for compilation of community and craft data used published sources, key informants, local government officials, teachers, businessmen, local leaders and residents, and included 100 craft-producing households. Anthropological methods of participant observation and extended interviews were also used, with supplementary photographic recordings. The researcher lived in a local household with residents employed in the crafts being studied.

Following the initial analysis, cases were chosen to study specific issues. Women in the case studies represent various household types (nuclear, extended, polygamous), family structures, life cycles, occupational and status groups. The cases are presented in order to show the relationship between women's choices and possibilities and their socio-economic and kinship positions, and to stress the complexity of these relationships.

The sample was not taken from all women in the village. Rather, only married women who were parents and who were employed in craft production were selected from the survey of 100 craft-producing households. These represent approximately 10 per cent of Kerdassa women thus occupied. Single-parent households and unmarried craftswomen were not represented. Further basic material and data were collected from this non-random sample by Fahmy, assisted by two bilingual village assistants, through three or four interviews with each informant, in focused interviews using a loosely structured questionnaire designed to be both acceptable and understood by Egyptian informants and acceptable for the survey.

The team worked closely together on the integration of the data into the final report, and were assisted by Nawal Hassan, Center Director, who was closely involved with the project at every stage from development to report compilation.

The Seven Roles of Women conceptual framework for data collection (Oppong, 1980; Oppong and Church, 1981) was used in the collection and organisation of data. This framework is comprehensive and flexible enough to allow a personal assimilation according to differences in theoretical orientation and is adaptable to the necessarily great number of issues and problems which are addressed. The focus is on occupational and parental roles, with some attention paid to conjugal and kin roles. In addition to the Anker (1980, 1981) survey questionnaires, we found Connel and Lipton's (1977) suggestions helpful in the collection of village information.

Questions were used to generate conversation on specific topics rather than to collect specific answers. The project depended heavily upon established long-term relationships with particular informants to gain trust, and most information was gathered from regular conversations carried out over a certain period. Hoda Fahmy's previous work and residence in the village proved valuable in this respect.

Criticism of method used

We found insights into the differences between members of the cross-cultural team interesting and valuable. The co-operation demanded close personal examination of motives, ideas, and theoretical assumptions, involving both project and individual aims. We feel that having to assess the data collection jointly as the project progressed and to discuss its import was of benefit to all concerned and to the outcome of the project.

The two village assistants came from a family in residence and proved to be invaluable. Without them it would have taken much longer to gain access to and the trust of informants. The fact that we were unable to find bilingual female assistants did change the character of relationships between Lynch and women in the village somewhat, especially before she was able to speak fluent Arabic. Even though informants usually knew the assistants and, in some cases were related to them, the nature of conversation between members of a mixed group is somewhat limited. Hoda Fahmy's cultural as well as linguistic knowledge was a great asset in the collection of information on attitudes. Lynch's married status and her position as a mother helped somewhat to mitigate this problem as it increased rapport with, and the trust of, women in the village.

We found two problems with the use of local, untrained assistants, although we would not hesitate to use them again. Lack of training in field methods caused a communication gap which sometimes surfaced during interviews. However, through this we learned to review questions and topics for both cultural and courtesy suitability. A class problem occurred which, as we questioned many households besides those presented as case studies, surfaces as a general one in the collection of village data. Assistants felt able to ask any question, personal or otherwise, of a poorer producer, not finding this an invasion of the informant's privacy. They found it more difficult, however, to ask any questions of informants from higher status groups than their own. Within the family in residence we also found difficulty in obtaining answers to questions on financial matters, although some could be found through observation. Long residence in the village helped us to gain information about household maintenance, land use, etc.

We noted that many aspects of women's responsibilities are difficult for them to discuss; for example, certain tasks which have low status within the community. Manual labour generally is not prized, nor is routine, unskilled craft work. Men deny that wives perform these tasks even when their own work depends upon them and cannot be completed without the participation of their wives. Women will not admit to performing these tasks unless observed in the process of carrying them out: then they will talk about them.

Surveys are difficult because of the time it takes to gain trust and to evaluate informants and answers. When informants do not know the questioner or his reasons for asking, they often give incorrect information.

For all these reasons, much information was gained through observation. We did find the questionnaire by Anker (1980) useful in the collection of basic data about households, family structure, facilities, activities and income. Its design for a full year's project, while not precisely the pattern of this research, was also helpful.

Because only marriage and childbearing are sources of status for women and work outside or inside the home for money is not, women are not anxious to discuss the latter. This is especially true of subsistence crafts, which have the lowest status, or where women perform tasks for much needed remuneration which they consider below their social status. They prefer to hide the fact that they do this work. In this case questionnaires, however well thought out and extensive, fail.

There is also a certain bias in the work because of the privileged position of most key informants. These included members of the village council, government officials, professionals, merchants, and other educated people. These are of necessity over-represented in the collection of community data. Members of families with whom Lynch resided are extensively used as sources of information and these were not among the poorer families. They were closely related to the leading village merchant, who provided much information on local production, but we know the issue of family loyalties was inescapable and that both political and class issues between families, as well as personal ones, prevented us in some cases from gaining an "objective" view of production and marketing, if such exists. We feel that the roots of this family in the traditional weaving industry and its prominent position in the tourist trade provided us with benefits which far outweighed drawbacks. Without their kind and patient assistance and care, the study could not have been carried out.

APPENDIX II

The cases–eleven women craft workers

It should be noted that the names of the eleven women craft workers have been changed.

Amina

Amina is a thoughtful young wife and mother. She has a refreshing cynicism and an unusual ability to view life in a wider context, which made her an informative subject. We also chose her because she signifies much of the change taking place in Kerdassa as it moves from a specialising village into the grip of a capitalist urban-centred international market.

Her house lies in the very oldest section of the village above the flood plain where weavers clustered in bygone times. Most of the interior has been torn down and is being rebuilt little by little. At present, only three rooms remain, which house Amina and her husband Ahmed, their two small daughters, and his parents. Amina is twenty-four and has been married for four years. Neither she nor Ahmed have ever attended school. Ahmed was trained in weaving by his father and had worked in this craft since he was a child. Recently, he has been employed by a nearby television and radio factory, where he earns LE 25 per month, plus overtime and profit-sharing bonuses.

Ahmed's father, Abdel Salaam, is respected both for his good character and because he is a weaver, an occupation which retains some status from former times when it was a lucrative trade which occupied most of the village. He weaves very good quality cotton tea towels on the small pit loom which occupies half the front room, and he sells these to a merchant in the centre of Gamaleya, the ancient bazaar area of Cairo. He is proud of his work, but worries that he is getting old, can no longer work long days, and is only able to earn about LE 1 for two days' work, out of which he must pay for dyes. This fee also includes the help of his wife, a small, bent woman who is nevertheless lively and who keeps busy helping Abdel Salaam by winding bobbins and dyeing the yarn red, black, and yellow. The technology used by the couple is simple but highly effective.

Abdel Salaam also worries that the merchant is trying to cheat him on the price of his tea towels and asks me to check on the sale price. It is difficult for him to pay for cotton and dyes from his earnings, and he also finds it increasingly hard to travel the very long way on the crowded bus, then on foot, to sell his tea towels and to buy new yarn.

Because her husband no longer works in the house as a weaver, Amina does not help him in his work. She cooks, launders, and cleans for the whole family, which takes a lot of time because of the conditions of the house, and she must walk a considerable distance with water from the public tap. She goes twice a week to her father's house nearby to bake bread in his oven and she enjoys visiting her mother and family members, which she feels she is more free to do now since Ahmed is not at home to watch her movements so closely. Her mother-in-law minds the baby and young daughter when she is on errands, which helps her, but she sometimes prefers to take them with her.

Neither side of the family owns land, and Amina does not keep animals, chickens, or ducks, and is not involved in processing food such as dates or corn for the household. She has searched very hard for some sort of income-producing work and is discouraged about her inability to find anything she feels is worth the time she puts in or which she can do. She used to sew gold beads on *galabeya* bodices for local women, but gave it up as she did not feel the LE 1.25 was worth the two days of spare-time work which was involved. She still does it for the members of her extended family, however, as she is quite good at it. She also enrolled in a sewing course given by the Ministry of Social Affairs, but found the training in canvas embroidery (petit point) had little relation to her real work needs and so she stopped attending this course. She regrets this in a way, however, because if she had stayed to finish, they would have helped her to purchase a sewing machine on credit, which she would like very much to do. Then she could become a tailor, which is the only skill she has. She has no capital or credit to buy the machine on her own, and the demands of her children and household duties prevent her from selling things in the local market. Besides, she has no land to grow things to sell.

Amina's eldest child is 2 years and two months, and her two pregnancies correspond with her actual number of children. She was registered at the government clinic for both pregnancies because she thought it would be wiser in case she had a pre- or post-partum haemorrhage and needed a doctor quickly. She does not intend to be registered for her next pregnancy because "it is useless", and she did not go for check-ups while pregnant. When delivery was near she sent for the *daya* (midwife) and went to her mother's home, where she gave birth. Her two deliveries were easy and the *daya* managed well.

When her children become ill she takes them to the public clinic but says that they do nothing for them and above all she has no trust in them as she feels doctors in the public clinic are not specialised in childcare and "they prescribe for children what they would prescribe for adults". When her youngest daughter was sick she took her to a private doctor and paid LE 1 for the visit.

When asked if she wanted more children Amina at first said no, that she had quite enough, but she later admitted that she wanted to have a son. "It is not possible to be satisfied with only two daughters, I wish to have one boy at least." Her husband is always asking her, "When are you going to give me a boy?" and her in-laws also press her constantly on the issue. She is actually worried that she will not be able to have more children as she has passed a year without getting pregnant. She is also afraid she might have a third daughter and thinks it would not be good for them not to have a brother to protect them. She has heard about some contraceptive devices like the pills and the loop and says that if God gives her a satisfactory number of children she will use the loop in future. She has heard the pill causes bleeding and affects the liver, but feels the loop is safe as relatives in Imbaba seem satisfied with it. No one from the family planning clinic has ever visited her, but she heard about the need for limiting births from the radio, from television, and from her neighbours.

Amina thinks it is especially important to educate her children well as she suffers from being "only a housewife". Education is an important tool to develop one's personality and to help in finding an occupation which will bring a fixed income each month. "Children are a support in life", she says, although she adds with some cynicism, "one educates, gets tired, makes sacrifices for one's children and in the end the mother gets nothing back as the girls get married and leave the house and perhaps they may never ask about their parents after they have gone".

She considers her in-laws helpful and kind and is happy to live with them, actually preferring this to living in a nuclear unit. She is also quite happy with her husband, who has many positive qualities, including kindness, modesty, treating his children well and fulfilling both her and the children's wishes. She has an increased sense of security since he took a job outside the house with a fixed work period and income, and enjoys the freedom and responsibility this gives her. She tries to please him by doing extra tasks like helping him with building and carrying sand for him. She is glad they have electricity in the house but wishes she did not have to carry water such a long way, and she complains about the exhaustion this causes as she must do it several times each day. She tries not to feel annoyed about the housework, as she realises her parents-in-law are old and need help, and there is no other female to assist.

Amina is very preoccupied these days by the idea that she must contribute to raising the income of the family by taking on some kind of work. The problem for her is what can she do? It would give her a sense of security and fulfillment to have money which she could spend in any way she liked. She sees that sewing and embroidery are no longer lucrative in Kerdassa and she is seeking some income-generating and self-rewarding activity which her commitments and skills will allow her to do.

Safeya

Safeya is a woman with a strong personality, a strong reproductive role, and a prominent productive life. I have never seen her when she has not been working, yet she is always cheerful, alert, and hospitable. She lives under what appear to be difficult and austere circumstances, which in no way dampen her spirit or her enthusiasm for life. Safeya is 33 years old and was married for 15 years to Sha'rawy, a *versalia* merchant (who died as we were carrying out our research). She was Sha'rawy's obviously favoured second wife and the mother of six children, three sons and three daughters, the eldest of which was 14 years. Sha'rawy was 53 and had been married to Atiat for about 15 years before he brought Safeya to their home. Atiat had only one surviving child at that time, a son, and has since had another daughter. Safeya acts very much the mistress of the polygamous household, a role which Atiat seems to accept gracefully, at least to all outward appearances, and we note in our family photograph that the co-wives stand together and Safeya affectionately rests her arm on Atiat's shoulder.

Sha'rawy's family has been weavers for a long time, and his father is still active and productive. Sha'rawy and his three brothers occupy a large compound near the centre of the village where they work and live. About 15 years ago the family decided to enter *versalia* production as a replacement for the declining handloom industry. As they were also cloth merchants, they used their considerable links in the old Cairo bazaar to gain new customers for this work, which is linked to the bespoke clothing and luggage industry. Since then the handloomed *versalia* has been replaced by machine-made products which are ordered from Alexandria merchants. In Safeya's household, production is entirely carried out by women, including her co-wife, the wife of her father-in-law, Atiat's 12-year old daughter, and the younger

61

girls when needed. After his first wife died, her father-in-law married a woman of about 50 years from an adjoining village and with the other women, she shares the tasks of getting the starch prepared in large ceramic pots over a fire, stirring the cloth into the hot starch, then lifting it out with a stick to stretch on the nail-lined roof racks to dry in the hot sun. The work is heavy and dirty and is done twice each day, taking two or more hours at a time. The women must rise early, especially in the short days of winter, to get one load dried so that it can be removed and rolled for storage before another is put out to dry and then removed before dusk.

The house is large with an open central court, three rooms on the ground floor and one above. Most of these are used for materials and for storage. There are 82 metres of drying racks on the roof and *versalia* is made in the court and carried up the stairs or to neighbouring roofs to dry. Sha'rawy's only role in the industry was to manage business affairs, arrange shipment to the city, collect money for the work, and take new orders. He also obtained supplies and materials. There are four *versalia* merchants in the village who distribute the work of many households, and even at the small profit of 2 piastres (2 piastres = 3 cents American) per metre for starching, a good profit can be made. Sha'rawy estimated for us that he sold 200 *tobe* (1 tobe = 32 metres) to the city each week, which included the output of several neighbours.

He and his brothers do not collaborate in their work; rather each brother produces and markets for himself. This competition is characteristic of Kerdassa, even where combined and co-ordinated efforts might be a financial benefit or help to develop a small business. The tendency for brothers to compete often leads to family friction. Although there are no outward signs of conspicuous consumption in the household, village informants insist that Sha'rawy is "wealthy". This may be because of his constant income due to the strong demand for this product that is linked to wider market production, and because of Sha'rawy's control of this village speciality. In 1977 Sha'rawy and his father travelled to Mecca, a fact proclaimed by the customary bright wall paintings in his house done by neighbours to welcome them home. He took his sister, but did not include Safeya, although she wanted to go.

Safeya is a small, wiry woman, and her wizened breasts seem inadequate for nursing Sabat, 2, who is not a robust child like the young Sha'rawy, who at one year older was his father's obvious favourite. Partly because of the hard nature of the work, it is difficult for Safeya to spend a lot of time caring for her young children, and they are very boisterous. The household contains a water pump and it has electricity, although standards of sanitation are not high. They do not keep any animals or fowl, but do own a tiny plot of land which supplies dates to the household. The co-wives claim to share equally in the housework, but we note that Atiat and her daughter seem to bear much of the load of routine household tasks, leaving Safeya free to travel to the city to deliver goods and collect new orders, and to sell fabric in the weekly *suq*. We often saw her there with her wares spread out in a prominent place just outside the gates to the "new" *suq*, and accompanied by Sha'rawy who visited with his friends while she worked. We observed that the wives did not share the same lifestyle as their husband, nor have the same decision-making power over how the family income would be spent, what work they did, or what leisure they had. Safeya was provided with little above subsistence. Sha'rawy controlled her movements and she checked her plans with him at each step. Although he was often seen with his small son, Sha'rawy admitted he liked to get away from the noisy and chaotic household, and he was considered by informants to be a very hard man. Sha'rawy had paid a brideprice of

LE 20 for his first wife, and a price of LE 40 for Safeya, prices which reflect change over time if compared with the younger women in the study.

The shock of Sha'rawy's sudden death from asthma was very hard on the family, although Safeya had taken over much of the business some time before because of his failing health. We were curious to see whether male members of the extended family would allow the women to continue supporting themselves, or whether Sha'rawy's father would assume a managerial role. Women in the village usually fall under the care of a male extended family member. We also wondered what would happen to the polygamous household.

In our following visits we noted that Safeya continued both her selling in the weekly *suq* and her *versalia* business, with the help of her mother who came for a visit, and her co-wife, whom Safeya said she would never leave. She discussed how she accomplished her own autonomy by separating herself from "jealous" members of her husband's family, and how she was able to take only two weeks off after Sha'rawy's death because she feared customers would turn elsewhere for supplies. She says that the money "is the same as before for me and my children" and seems very happy about control of funds, with which she is prone to be ostentatious.

Safeya is inclined to idealise her life with Sha'rawy, which affects her attitudes toward children. In all she has had 14 pregnancies, with two children born alive and dying within the first year, six spontaneous abortions, and six surviving children. She does not know of any specific reason for these deaths, but said that God had summoned them to be near him and had compensated with other children. She noted that they had severe diarrhoea, however. All the children were delivered at home, which she considers preferable to the hospital. She was assisted by the *daya*, in this case a very old woman who is nearly blind but who has had many years experience. Her deliveries were very easy so she could resume normal life after two or three days, during which time her co-wife and neighbours assisted her. One of the six abortions was extremely difficult and she haemorrhaged badly and thought she was going to die. The *daya* suggested she should immediately go to a hospital, so neighbours rushed her to "Om El Musreyyin" in Cairo.

She is registered at the government clinic, where there is a big difference, she says, between the services rendered today and those of 15 years ago. The clinic used to dispense medicine without charge, but now they give very little, not exceeding one or two sorts, and all consultations were verbal as no one cared to examine patients in the overcrowded clinic. Despite this, she thinks the public clinic is "better than nothing" as she claims she cannot pay the 75 piastres for a private doctor. Despite her lack of pre-natal care she "never had any problems" with pregnancies. When her children or husband were seriously ill she preferred to go to a public hospital in Cairo where better care is given, free of charge.

When Sha'rawy was alive Safeya says she never thought of controlling the size of her family or of using any kind of contraceptive. She was very happy to have children and said that each child brings his *rizk* (prosperity) with him. Safeya was very conscious of the fact that her husband took her as a second wife because he wanted to have many children and his first wife was already "very old". Her opinion coincided with his and she says that now the best memory she has of her husband is her children. They also help her in her productive role; "with many children a woman feels supported and not alone". She thinks that, as long as her health allows, a woman should have as many children as she can, especially as many die natural deaths or are aborted, as happened in her case and "one can never be sure of the number of children who will survive". Her husband was happy when she was pregnant and never suggested that they had too many children. She heard about contraceptive pills from some village women, not from the government clinic, and knew that they took away a woman's energy and might affect her productivity, which is very important to her. She never found the clinic helpful for anything except administering vaccinations to village children.

Safeya thinks that education is good for her children, and especially her two elder sons, who are 14 and 12 years old. Now that Sha'rawy is dead she thinks it is enough to educate the boys only, and has even had to take her eldest son out of school to help her in the business. She hopes to teach her children to be strong and responsible very early in their lives, as her mother taught her when she was a small child and she took her to sell vegetables in the streets of Cairo where she "learned independence". This is why she now feels capable of assuming the role of both mother and father for her children. She thinks education is more useful for boys than for girls because girls marry and usually become involved in the work of their husbands as in her own case. She does not want the boys to lack education as their father did, or to work in crafts, but would prefer they have work for a fixed income. She would like her children to be better off than she is and not to suffer from poverty as she does, but also to be as courageous in facing life as she tries to be. She recognises the good care which Atiat takes of her children, which allows her to feel secure while she is carrying out her marketing activities.

She hopes to be financially independent of her children, but if the need arises she expects them to assist her when they get older, "of course more from the boys", as girls will be financially dependent upon their husbands. In her view, Sha'rawy was a good companion and she knows that she was his preferred wife, but has no trouble accepting that he married her because she was clever in business. She did resent the fact that her husband controlled all the money, including what she earned, and was the sole decision-maker, which especially annoyed her because she worked so hard. She could not buy anything she needed for herself or her children. However, she did find some reward in seeing him pleased with his work and affectionate towards the children.

Safeya desires greatly to be financially independent from her in-laws and says her only link with them is her children. Although she feels it is their duty to help support her now that she is a widow, she tries to prevent the children from asking them for money as she fears they will attempt to control her business and her money. She feels that her role is outside the house, in producing and marketing goods, rather than in the house. She enjoyed preparing the vegetables in front of the television on her one day off, but found the demands of providing so much clean laundry for Sha'rawy difficult, as she was compelled to rise very early to get it done. She likes *versalia* production and finds market day her greatest joy. Because of the poverty she suffered when she was young she feels that learning about life, earning money and knowing the market gives her a source of security in life. She feels that marketing is "in her blood" and has liked it since she was a child and marketed with her mother. She regards herself successful in her work and capable of running the business. It is because of her confidence and success that she fears the neighbours and her in-laws will give her the "evil eye" which will bring her bad luck. She hopes her daughters will also find satisfaction in the future in the two roles in which she herself feels rewarded, as a mother and as a producer.

Amal

Amal is a buxom, pretty young woman who has a business of her own as a tailor of the traditional female dress in Kerdassa, the "baladi" *galabeya*. She is 27, has been married to Nasr (36 years) for eight years and has two children, a son of six and a daughter 1½. The family lives in a very large, prominent house which belongs to her mother, although they have separate quarters. Nasr is unusual in this respect because he is one of the few to violate the rule of virilocality and it is for this reason and because of their interesting family and class backgrounds that we have chosen to look more closely at Amal.

Their spacious home has high ceilings and stone floors and contains a separate *salon* with cushioned *canaba* where guests can be entertained. The *wist al bait* also has a tiled floor and opens onto a garden which separates Amal's living quarters from her mother's. The formidable wooden entrance is high above the street and the door is kept bolted. Her single brother shares the home and travels to work in the city. The house has running water, electricity, and an oven, although Amal seldom bakes her own bread, preferring to purchase it from the baker. She does not raise animals, although she does occasionally keep chickens for family consumption. There is a television set and a washing machine. She purchases fuel (dung cakes) when needed, rather than making them, and is very proud of the fact that she purchases everything she needs for the house rather than making it herself. The family has no land except for a small plot in her name, although Nasr's family owned much property in the past.

Amal works hard as a tailor, sewing for about four hours in the shorter winter days and about seven hours in summer. Her work tends to be seasonal, as most women buy new dresses for the "small feast" or for Ramadan and for two months prior to this time she is very busy, making three or four per day. The rest of the year her production is about three in two days. Women bring their fabric to Amal and she sews it according to their choice from a variety of local styles, making about 70 piastres to LE 1.50 for each one, depending upon the work involved. She has no particular training for this job so finishing skills are not very well developed, although this does not seem to affect her business very much. After she assembles the dress it is taken to another tailor for machine embroidery or hand-beading on the finely finished bodice.

Amal measures her customers against the cloth they bring, making notches with her scissors which she will follow after they leave and which guide her in cutting the bodice, sleeves, body and bottom ruffle. Sleeves are not added until the customer comes to collect the *galabeya*, and adjustments are made. Each woman has her own favourite style, fabric, trimming and yoke design. Because of the nature of the work it is difficult for Amal's husband to know just how much she earns, and when she says that she uses the money for household expenses he complains that this is not so. He says she contributes nothing to the house and is always asking him for money which she keeps for herself. Amal laughs at this and seems unconcerned. This point of conflict between them may be accentuated because of the strong position Amal holds in relation to her husband and also because she is able to conceal the amount of her income from him.

Both Amal and Nasr come from prominent families. His father was a village strongman whose family was once the primary landholder in the village. He is related to the last *omda* (mayor) and the family was very powerful before this office was abolished by Nasser in 1965. Nasr rejected the tendency of his father to take what he wanted by force and now works as a mechanic on the construction of a giant hotel complex in Giza on a fertile 20-*feddan* plot which was once controlled by his family. Because he refused to help his father get a job on this building project, his father has disowned him and disinherited him. He has, therefore, "married in", so to speak and has broken all ties with his family.

Amal's mother lived for many years in Cairo, where her first husband was in a prominent position in the Ministry of Education. After his death she returned to her family home in Kerdassa and married a weaver of simple means, but later separated from him and now lives with her son in her father's house. She speaks some English and their home reflects their higher status. Her sister is married to a prominent Minister and Amal's sister works for him and lives with him in the city. Her cousin lives in New York, so family ties beyond the village are strong. Status here means access to power as well as to economic position, and this gives Amal an enviable position in relation to her husband, who does not have family backing in exerting his authority over her. Her economic independence adds to this situation. Men in the village often express a distrust of women who have independent incomes and say they do not need their husbands and will desert them if they are unhappy.

Her family position is also one of the reasons she is able to be active in an independent wage-earning occupation, because without her mother's or husband's cash or credit she could not purchase a sewing machine and other comforts which allow her sufficient time to devote to her work. Nevertheless, Nasr approves of her job because he feels she would otherwise be bored, with no animals to care for. Standards of cleanliness in this household are the highest we encountered in the village and both children are very clean and well fed. Amal and her husband both look strong, healthy, and of above average size.

Although Amal did not register at the public clinic she has had no trouble with either pregnancy; "they were so easy I did not have to go to a private doctor or to a hospital". In both cases the deliveries took place in her mother's home with the *daya* attending her and with her mother helping and caring for her afterward. During the second pregnancy she suffered some bleeding and tiredness, and because she was worried, decided to visit a private physician for a check-up and vitamins. When her children are sick she always takes them to a private doctor. She considers her time too precious to wait in the crowded public clinic and prefers to pay the fee of 75 piastres to be received immediately so that she is not kept away from her work.

Amal thinks that her present number of children is sufficient especially as both parents are working and wish to educate and care for them properly. She feels that her productive role is very important and if she were to have more children, would be obliged to neglect her work. However, her husband thinks that two more children would be ideal. Amal feels that she should be the one to decide this issue since she is the one who has to do all the housework and shoulder the burden of raising the children, taking on the additional household duties. Men contribute nothing but money to their care, she feels, and should "by no means" decide the number of children a wife will have. The high status of Amal's family and Nasr's poor position in relation to hers because he is cut off from family backing, combine to keep Nasr in an unfavourable bargaining position and his decision-making power is thus decreased in relation to hers. To date, Amal's decisions have been taken into consideration in this difference of opinion, a second source of family conflict.

Amal has heard about pills, the loop, and the condom as contraceptive devices and she took the pill to space her pregnancies, however, she is now under pressure from Nasr to stop. In her opinion the pill represents the safest method, as with a loop a woman may still become pregnant if the loop becomes misplaced and she is not prepared to take this risk. Amal said that the public clinic does nothing to help women who are practising family planning, although it sells pills for 45 piastres per strip "with added vitamins". She is conscious that not everyone can afford this much. As she is in both cases obliged to pay for her medication, she thinks a private doctor costs the same as the clinic, as it also saves time.

Amal feels that a university education is important for girls as well as boys in order that they feel "not less than anyone else". Education and especially a university certificate is her first priority for her children. She thinks it wrong to assume that girls are to be married and stay at home, but says it is "even more important" for girls to work. If a girl works before marriage and continues this after marriage her husband and in-laws will respect her more and will hesitate to criticise and offend her. She feels her daughter would not then be "overly obedient" to her husband in an exaggerated way as is often seen in couples where the woman needs financial support from her husband or is completely dependent upon him. Being independent, with her own source of income through work, makes a woman feel psychologically at ease and the relationship with her husband becomes freer in the sense that she does not feel submissive. Amal wants to establish these values in the mind of her daughter.

Amal hopes that her children can have a better life than she has had. She is sorry she did not go to school or to university and was at times obliged to beg for financial assistance when her family was going through a difficult period. She hates the feeling of having to ask for money even from her husband. She is very happy with her work, her parents, and her children, but regrets the conflict with her husband and feels she "does not owe him much respect" as she considers him egotistic. He spends very little on their children and feels threatened by the fact that she is using her income to build a house of her own on a half *kirat* of land she bought and registered in her name. She puts her earnings aside in a box each day so that she may begin building and works hard to save as much as she can. This has become her primary aim.

However, this is not the only reason she works, as money is not a reward in itself. She would work "even if she were rich". Work makes her happy and satisfied and helps her to forget the world. It is a source of reward and equilibrium in her life. Thus, she avoids anything that would interrupt her work, such as having additional children.

Amal feels proud and happy that she is known in Kerdassa for her capacity to do neat work and, in order to keep her high standards, she purchases the best equipment. She has two types of sewing machine, each for specialised functions. She relies on her mother to help her a lot and to relieve her from the duties of childcare and housework that would interrupt her; her appliances also make this easier. She finds her roles as mother and producer the ones which are most rewarding and finds that her purchasing food makes her feel nearer to city women and not like a "baladi" woman, which she does not want to be. She would have liked to live in Cairo, yet feels the bad housing conditions would have prevented her from living in a house as pleasant as the spacious one her family now occupies.

Halima

Halima is a beautiful and respected young woman of 28 years. She is considered polite, uncomplaining, hardworking, and obedient, all highly valued traits in the village. Her husband Mustafa, who is 33, has been married to her for 11 years and works as a storekeeper for the chief textile merchant in the village. They occupy a very small, two-roomed house owned by the merchant. Water is available from a pump next to the house, and she has electricity inside, but she must use her neighbour Hanim's oven or bake her bread at her father's house nearby.

Halima works very hard to keep her home and her children clean and tidy, always sweeping, washing the grass mat in the alley, and scrubbing clothes. This is a difficult task in this older area of town, but she succeeds admirably, and sanitation standards for her family are well above average.

Halima has barely recovered from a depression following the tragic accident last summer in which her 5-year old daughter was injured playing with fire and subsequently died. Two months later she lost an infant son, and she has lost another son in the past. Her three remaining children are very precious to her and she watches them very closely. Her two elder sons, 12 and 10 years, both go to school and her daughter, Himat, can always be seen at her mother's side or in her arms. Her sons are unusually polite and well mannered for village boys, who are often precocious. The family is softly spoken and treat each other with respect. Mustafa is known to be a quiet, good man who cares a lot for his family. It is said that he was greatly loved by the father of his present employer and he worked for the family for a long time.

Before the accident, Halima used to produce large quantities of hand-embroidered "siwa" *galabeyas* for the merchant, usually finishing one each day. Cut-out *galabeyas* and yarn were supplied to her by the merchant and she was paid LE 2.50 for each one. During the past two years, however, the price for her labour has fallen drastically until now Halima only earns 60 piastres for each *galabeya*; thus she has reduced her production to one per week. Because her husband works for the leading merchant and because they live in a house which belongs to him, Halima cannot embroider *galabeyas* for the other shops which might pay her a little more for her work.

The money she earns from sewing, which she does "when she is not busy in the house", goes "into her pocket", she says. Although she first claimed that she used all of it for household expenses and not for herself, she later admitted that if she could accumulate enough she purchased gold jewellery. Halima does not keep any animals and does not own any land, although her father owns 8 *kirat*. She does all the household maintenance and food preparation for her own family and she often helps her elderly neighbour next door, who has no female to help her with her two grown sons and two grandchildren who usually stay with her. Halima tries to see that Hanim's water jar is filled and the floors are swept. When she uses Hanim's oven to bake her bread, she gives some of the bread to him.

The fathers of both Halima and Mustafa were weavers in the old area of the village. Halima's father had many looms producing shawls and headscarves, and he was a merchant as well as a producer. Mustafa's father was a *versalia* weaver of more simple means, but he was a good friend to her brother, who helped to promote the marriage. Halima's brothers and her sister were secondary school educated, although she herself never went to school. Two brothers work outside the village and one brother

68

still assists her father in weaving. Two other brothers are still at school. Mustafa had only five years schooling, but, although his salary is not high, he makes more than some government employees in the village, and his work is regular and stable. Mustafa paid a brideprice of LE 100 to Halima's parents.

They are a nuclear family, yet reside near both natal families and spend much time with them. Kinship links provide most of their relationships, including those of friendship, assistance, financing, and business. Halima is very sad that her sister is prevented by her mother-in-law from visiting with her, and feels this loss deeply as she has mostly brothers.

In all, Halima has been pregnant nine times; she had three spontaneous abortions and three children died in accidents or through dehydration. The local *daya* attended her during her six deliveries and she trusts this *daya,* whom she knows well and who is a neighbour. Two of the abortions took place in the child-care hospital in Cairo and the third abortion occurred at home with her neighbour/*daya* taking care of her. She had no problems with the abortion and has had no premature births. Halima had no medical supervision for her pregnancies and has never registered at the local clinic. She heard lots of advice from her neighbours and friends, but after the deaths of her three children she stopped taking their advice and also stopped administering "folk" treatments. She felt too embarrassed to go to a male doctor for a consultation. However, after the care she received during her abortion in the hospital in Cairo, she has decided that next time she is pregnant she will register at the child-care hospital there.

Halima refuses to answer the question "what is the ideal number of children you would like to have?" but continually invokes the name of God, saying "it is the will of God". She has never spoken with her husband about the ideal number of children they ought to have, but he is a religious man and is against family planning, saying that "one should not interfere with God's plan" and Halima would not like to sadden him. She has heard about the pill as a contraceptive device but has never thought of using it, especially now with the death of three babies, as she feels she is no longer young and would like to compensate for those that have died. Besides, she has heard that "all devices are bad".

She goes to the public clinic when she or one of her children is sick and was pleased that the examinations and medicine were free; now she has to pay for them. She would like it if they had a female doctor there as she feels it is against her religion to be examined by a man.

Education is more important for boys than for girls, Halima tells us, especially because university education helps boys to get a good job. A girl's education helps her more in terms of developing her personality as most girls stay at home after they marry and look after husbands and children. Halima does not have great ambitions for her life, but wishes to please her husband and to raise those children she has, well. Her main priority is to fulfil her role as wife and mother, teaching her children to be obedient, polite, quiet, tender and clean, values which she believes most important. They do, indeed, reflect this teaching, and bear out her avowal that she applies these values to her own life as well.

Although she is especially close to the elderly neighbour whom she helps with chores and who in turn assists her with her children, Halima generally prefers to carry out her household duties herself, without asking anyone for assistance. She wishes to stay at home most of the time, using her energy to serve her family rather than in visiting and chatting with other wives or family members. She complains that her house gets very dusty because it opens onto the street and requires much work. She likes baking bread and cooking best because she thinks they require creative skills and not everyone can succeed in preparing good bread or a fine meal. Her own creative approach to these tasks shows a deep involvement in them. She enjoys having her own house and not having to share it with in-laws as this makes her feel more free and enables her to enjoy staying at home.

She feels fulfilled in her role as wife and mother and does not require much from her husband. The qualities most important to her are that he respect her, appreciate what she does for him, treat her well and not beat her. He should spend his money on the house and the children. As he possesses these qualities, she considers him an ideal husband. In return she respects him and obeys him and tries in every possible way to please him, not burdening him with demands, especially monetary, which he cannot meet.

She tries hard to economise, and used to raise chickens so that she could sell them and their eggs. Her husband never asked her for the money she made, and if she needed it, she used it for the household, otherwise investing it in gold. She would like to be involved in some activity which could bring her income from working at home, but she would not consider working outside. *Galabeya* embroidery is no longer rewarding, but she would like something similar that she can do while watching television as she would prefer this to gossiping or chatting with neighbours. "It is better to be reserved and not to be interested in people or in talk, especially when it is directed to others". She may need money for her children in the future, as no one knows what the circumstances will be then. Meanwhile, she will not work outside as "a woman's choice should be for her house and children, first and last".

Nagua

Family pictures attest to Nagua's former stunning beauty, although at 27 and after repeated pregnancies she is still slim and pretty. She has a positive but quiet attitude and a good-natured disposition. Nagua and Hamed, who is 35, have been married 13 years and have four girls and a baby son, ranging from 10 to 1½. The girls have adopted their mother's confident air but they are cautious and quiet with strangers.

Nagua's new brick house is close to that of her mother-in-law and it is cosy, roomy, and pleasant. The small courtyard is walled in and so has an unusual amount of privacy, as one must knock before entering from the street. There is electricity in the house but water must be carried from next door and Nagua does not yet have an oven so borrows one from her neighbour to bake bread once or twice a week. She has a washing machine, a radio, and two furnished bedrooms which double as sitting rooms. The family has no land and Nagua keeps no animals except chickens.

Nagua embroiders "siwa" design *galabeyas* for her husband, who runs a very active cottage industry in this dress which originated in Kerdassa, although it borrows designs from the Siwa oasis. He uses female labour from the neighbourhood; both married and young unmarried women work for him, implementing his original designs, which he markets in Alexandria and in the tourist market in Cairo's Khan el Khalili. Hamed works in Cairo during the day as a mechanic and says he could earn extra by working afternoons in this business, but he prefers the designing which "suits his personality". It is obvious he enjoys this work as he takes a very artistic attitude towards it, spending much time explaining his Pharoanic and customary local motifs. He likes to design garments that will appeal to a particular type of customer or suit people that he knows. Hamed travels to Alexandria once a month to market his *galabeyas*, where he sells them for LE 5.50 and makes about LE 40 per month at this, after paying the women for their sewing and the cost of cloth and embroidery yarn. In Khan el Khalili he can only get LE 5 for the same *galabeyas* because of stiff competition from other local manufacturers and because merchants prefer inferior work if they can purchase it cheaper. In spite of this, they sell his *galabeyas* at a very high mark-up, sometimes for LE 15.

Hamed has trouble getting the local women to finish work on time. He supervises the work closely and if they have a problem they come to consult him. He does not pay Nagua for her production, which she thinks is correct because it is "all the same if she gets paid or not". In fact, she prides herself that she does not take money "as other women do", and anyway "it is all for the family". She knows that Hamed has no money nowadays because he has spent so much on the new house. She usually produces two *galabeyas* a week, which is not as many as she used to do before the increase of her family and the demands of so many small children. Sometimes if household problems come up she may only be able to make one *galabeya* in two weeks.

Nagua is considered by village informants to be a very hard worker and an obedient wife and good mother. Her natal family is of modest means, but respectable, religious, and conservative. Her father, uncle, and cousin are builders. Hamed is criticised in the village because his relatives feel he does not live up to the highest standards of Islamic male behaviour and is not as devoted to his family as he should be. We note some contradiction in this, as Hamed spends a good deal of time tutoring his daughters and has placed a blackboard in the *wist al bait* for this purpose. He is very proud of the achievements of Manaal, 10, who excels in schoolwork, and who is already very good at embroidery. She does some work for her father and a finer type of needlework for school projects. All their children of school age are at school and Nagla, who is 8, is *muhajiba,* that is, she wears the conservative Islamic headcover which is encouraged by her teacher and supported by the family.

Nagua has had no education and Hamed attended primary school. As a fringe benefit from the factory where he works the family has spent holidays in Alexandria. Both work very hard to increase the living standard of their family and they encourage their daughters to succeed at school, providing a home environment where this is possible. As Hamed earns about LE 40-50 per month at his regular job he is well paid by local standards. The bridewealth which he paid to Nagua's father was LE 200, a high rate for that time in comparison to amounts declared by other informants, if, indeed, these reflect real prices.

Nagua was married for three years before she became pregnant and although she was worried, her husband objected to her going to see a gynaecologist on religious grounds, advising her to "leave it to God's will". She respected his wishes, but when some neighbours advised her to put a large piece of wool near her vagina in order to keep it very warm, she tried this and has had five children with a natural space between each birth which she attributes to breastfeeding. Although she experienced easy pregnancies with no complications, she did experience tiredness. She did not register at the public clinic and is very vociferous in her preference for the *daya*. The *daya,* she says, has much more "experience" than the doctor and this makes her much "better".

For her first pregnancies, she was delivered at her mother's nearby house, but later gave birth in her own home with her mother in attendance. Neighbours also assisted and helped to care for her afterwards.

Nagua feels that six children is quite sufficient, but Hamed says this is "up to God". They would both like to have one more boy and then they would be very satisfied. She would have liked to have boys to start with rather than girls, but thinks this, too, is God's will. She has never used any contraceptive device, although she has heard about the pill, the loop, and the condom. It would make her husband very angry if she were to use any form of device as he thinks they are against God's will, so she accepts his wishes.

When her husband is ill he can go to a doctor paid for by his company, but she and the children go to the public clinic, except in very serious cases, when they go to the hospital. She complains that medicines are not always available but she likes the free consultations. She has heard about family planning devices from neighbours who told her that people visited their homes to inform them and they heard about them on the radio. She believes that even if a woman wants to use contraceptives, it is the man who is the obstacle.

Nagua holds firm opinions about child-rearing. She tries to keep her children from playing in the street and teaches them to be obedient and clean and to stay near the house. She thinks girls should not be educated beyond primary school as they should not "be bothered with" trying to find a job. She prefers her daughters to stay at home, although she wants them to be educated enough to read and write, in case they need to read official certificates, letters from husbands who travel abroad, etc. She values university education for boys and hopes that her sons will become doctors or engineers.

As Nagua "sacrifices her entire life for her children", she believes they should do something in return for her and the boys, especially, are obliged to help her financially when she needs it and when she gets old. She does not see any obligation for her daughters to do the same, as they will be financially dependent upon their families, and she hopes they will be content with their husbands and homes. If she needs money now, she asks her husband or borrows it from her brothers.

Nagua is happy with her own house and glad she does not have to live with her parents-in-law. She likes her husband very much and thinks that he likes her because she "doesn't make trouble with the neighbours or talk nonsense with them" but closes the door of her house and sits all day with her children. She enjoys household tasks like washing, sweeping, cooking, cleaning, washing the children, baking bread and raising animals, and she does these without assistance. Her greatest pride comes from seeing her children clean and this makes her husband proud of them and of her "in front of his family and the neighbours".

She usually embroiders *galabeyas* for two to three hours a day if she finishes her routine household and child-care tasks, and finds this satisfying in a number of ways. She likes to contribute to her husband's efforts, quoting the proverb, "two hands clap better than one", and finds that her husband appreciates her and respects her more because of her contribution. Her participation also saves the price of another worker who would have to be employed. The money this saves, they can spend on the house and on the children and provide more adequately for their needs. She also gets pleasure from the work itself, and "each time wishes to do better than the time before".

She thinks Hamed is a good man who spends his income on the house and children. If she had more money she would continue improving the house and purchase more clothing for herself and her family. She raises chickens because it is also a saving and they are more nourishing than the ones she could purchase.

Both Nagua and her husband try to be good Muslims and she is very proud that her young daughter wears the *hijab*. She is grateful that Hamed shows his appreciation towards her in his kind manner, never making insulting remarks to her or beating her as many other men do. His treatment of her makes her satisfied and happy.

Jihan

It took us some time after we met her husband to manage to speak with Jihan, who has adopted the conservative Islamic attire (*hijab*) and lifestyle and so is limited in her contact with strangers outside the family. We have chosen her for this reason and because she signifies a select few village women who are in a position to realise the cultural ideal not to work, expressed by many cases and informants. No woman works, they say, unless she has to. The fact that a woman works is an implicit acknowledgement that her husband cannot support her according to the patriarchal ideal, and neither husband nor wife desires this. As Jihan used to have a more prominent productive role in the past, we were also interested in her attitudes towards work.

Jihan has a secondary school certificate, rare in Kerdassa. This seems to have a correlation with being *muhajiba*, perhaps because education raises the consciousness of this social choice. There are many different reasons why women in Egypt prefer to do this and neither their reasons nor their behaviour is identical. Jihan and her sisters have chosen to withdraw into the household rather than play an active role in teaching women or in serving the female community in a wider sense. This choice seems to be more common for conservative Muslim women in Kerdassa, and as a phenomenon it is increasing. In a community where nearly all women dress "baladi" they are prominent by their nun-like attire.

Jihan is 21 and has been married to Suliman, 27, for three years. He is the son of her mother's brother and Jihan had only to move a few houses to her husband's family compound. She has one child, one year and four months, and is seven months pregnant with her second child. The family lives in a large nuclear unit at the edge of his family compound, which is sumptuous by local standards, although small. There is electricity and water in the house, a Butagas stove and a refrigerator. They have a television and an electric fan, a salon with gilt furniture, a coffee table and a carpet. The bedroom has a modern bed and a wardrobe.

Adjoining the house is Suliman's busy tailoring workshop, which employs him and two other full-time tailors, as well as two apprentices. One of these is a relative and one travels from the next village. All the men in Suliman's family are tailors. Suliman works mostly for the leading merchant, who is related to him, but as he owns his own machines and shop he is free to sell to other merchants if he wishes, although kinship ties inhibit this somewhat. He has just moved from a small shop in the centre of the village to one adjoining the house, and he has the newest and most professional tailoring equipment, including three Japanese heavy-duty commercial sewing machines with large motors, cutting tables, etc. His layout is efficient for fast production, which is his speciality. The merchant supplies cloth and trimming and

73

Suliman is paid for each *galabeya* he produces. He can finish and decorate a *galabeya* in one and a quarter hours unless the power fails, which is frequent. He is responsible for designing many of the new styles seen in local shops, but he can also copy those styles coming into the village from the city. Skills gained over a lifetime in the family business have helped him to turn out work noted for its fine quality.

Jihan used to work about half a day with Suliman, "helping" him to trim *galabeyas* with beads or sequins, or assisting "as she was needed", but "doesn't find much time to do this now" since the birth of her baby. Suliman did not teach her to do the skilled jobs of cutting, sewing by machine, or finishing garments. Nowadays, she works actively inside the house, cleaning, washing, cooking, baking and caring for the baby. She appreciates the appliances which make her life easier, especially as she dislikes cleaning. She wants to raise chickens at home but considers that there is not enough space.

Jihan comes from a family which is considered "rich", and her mother, especially, is thought to be a strong and respected woman who has retained some status from her Turkish origins. All her six married sisters are *muhajiba*, and one sister has obtained a university degree although she also stays at home. There is land on both sides of the family. Her husband's family has 8 *feddans* on which they raise dates and fruit. His brothers share the use of a donkey. Suliman has a *diploma machina* from the technical high school, and a younger brother has just completed secretarial training, working as a tailor of men's trousers in his spare time. He is building a new house adjoining Jihan's and says when it is finished "any woman will come" and he can then marry. Jihan's brothers have good jobs both in and outside the village. When Jihan and Suliman became engaged he gave her LE 300 in gold, and at their marriage she received LE 1,000 in bridewealth.

Jihan did not get pregnant for 18 months after marriage, and this worried her very much. She went to a gynaecologist who performed minor surgery which allowed her to become pregnant quickly. Her actual number of children coincides with her pregnancies. She did not intend to become pregnant immediately after her first baby, and thought she could not as she was breastfeeding. However, she now feels very happy to be pregnant again and is looking forward to the new baby.

Her first delivery was very difficult. The *daya* in attendance asked the family to call a doctor when she found the case "delicate", so the husband of one of her sisters was summoned to assist her delivery. It was not a premature birth. She did not register at the public clinic and did not have a pre-natal check during her first pregnancy, but she thinks that delivery may have been difficult because of her failure to have medical care, so is under the supervision of a private doctor for this pregnancy. When anyone in her family falls ill they go to a private doctor, often her brother-in-law.

Jihan would like to have "only" three or four children as she wants to educate them and because life is becoming very expensive. Suliman is very "busy" and "does not have time to discuss such matters" with her, although they did agree on this while they were engaged. She has heard about the pill, the loop, and the condom. In the future when she has had all the children she wants, she plans to use the loop, as she feels the pill is bad for one's health and makes a woman very fat. Her husband told her that family planning was her responsibility and not his. She never went to the public clinic because she can afford a private doctor, but says that nothing is done to educate women about family planning. Women spread false rumours to one another, which she thinks is bad, or prescribe folk treatments. Although she believes girls are affectionate and tender, she would like to have at least one boy to carry on his father's name.

She regrets that she was not able to attend a university as her sister did because her parents "married her". She would like her daughter to be educated to university level in order to fulfil what she was not able to do herself. However, she does not see a university degree as a tool for obtaining work outside the house, which she feels is inappropriate for women. She thinks that Islam does not encourage women to seek work outside their homes and that they cannot properly carry out household responsibilities if they work outside as this makes too many demands on them. This is especially true if a woman has children to care for and a house to run. Rather, a university degree develops a woman's personality and increases her knowledge, which makes her respected among others and which enables her to discuss many issues with her husband and his acquaintances. This makes a husband proud of his wife.

Jihan thinks that children are one's greatest support. She confides everything to her mother and hopes her daughter will do the same. If God gives her a boy she would like him to marry and live in the house with her. "Of course a mother should rely on her sons when she gets old. This is the least they can do in return for what she has done for them." Boys are important, she says, although they are less affectionate than girls, because they carry their father's name and can inherit, which "girls cannot do according to Islamic Law". We took special note of this misinterpretation of the law and suspect this is because local practice often contradicts the law of inheritance.

Jihan likes to cook, and this is the only household task she finds rewarding. She worries because her husband works very hard and very long hours, and likes to be sure that he eats well. She appreciates that he never scolds her, although she sometimes neglects the house now because she feels tired. He treats her with great respect and, in her view, gives her considerable freedom, such as allowing her to decide what they will eat. She is glad she has a separate residence and does not live in her in-laws' house. She thinks her husband agrees that they can now afford for her to devote her time to looking after the baby and the house as he can employ workers in his shop. She does not believe that a husband respects or appreciates a wife because she assists him in his work, but only because she is a good wife, who is obedient, educated, and cares for him. She herself does not value work other than housework, but is content and fulfilled in her roles as a wife and mother. Her family position and "wealth" and her household appliances further contribute to her feeling of pride and contentment. She does not wish for more. We note that her pregnancies have improved her formerly tenuous position within the extended family, and this will be even more secure if her next birth produces a son.

Samira

Samira came to Kerdassa five years ago when she married Abdel Latif, who is a prominent tapestry weaver. She is now 25 and has three daughters, 4, 3, and 1½. Abdel Latif is also from outside the village but came here as a teenager from Sharkeya province to work in the new tourist industry. Neither has relatives in Kerdassa, and this places them in a somewhat different position from other case studies.

Samira lives in an old workshop which is owned by the leading merchant, and which contains six tapestry looms on the first floor and a bedroom for apprentices. Two new rooms have been added to the large, flat roof, where the family resides. There is water and electricity in the house although she must carry water upstairs. Samira complains a great deal because of the dangerous conditions under which she lives. There is no rail around the roof, and she must watch her small daughters each minute to be sure they do not venture too near the edge. This is a constant worry and restricts her movements greatly. There is an oven in the house, but she buys her bread. She has a Butagas stove and a washing machine. She keeps no animals or fowl, and her family has no land.

Samira did not go to school, but Abdel Latif had eight years of education. His father and grandfather before him were weavers in Sharkeya and he learned to weave *kelim* rugs and tapestries as an apprentice to his father. His identity is very closely aligned with his work, which he loves, and he says he was born under a loom, and the work is "his soul". Although the house and looms are owned by the merchant, Abdel Latif runs them and is responsible for teaching and recruiting weavers, as well as weaving himself. He works between seven and ten hours daily and dyes most of the wool used in his shop. He considers himself an artistic weaver and is proud of the fact that he uses only Egyptian materials. Five workers live and work in the house. One is an unmarried brother, and two are apprentices between 12 and 15, who are, he says, "better than sons". Even when he is smoking his water pipe and visiting, he gets up and down to check looms and the progress of the weavers, or to begin a new design. As they are paid per square metre of production they have an incentive to work quickly. In this shop production is very high and may reach five and a quarter square metres per month per worker (the average is two square metres). Prices are negotiated for each piece according to quality of design and finish, and each carpet is carefully assessed by the merchant who discusses each colour or change with Abdel Latif. In this way they decide what future products should be ordered.

As Abdel Latif controls six of the approximately 15 tapestry looms in the village, this puts him in a prominent place in the industry, for which the village is noted, and thus he earns an above average wage. All material inputs, including loom warping, which is done by a specialist, are supplied by the merchant. Designs and quality vary from rather poor to very good, depending on the skill of the weaver and his experience, but the large tapestries produced by Abdel Latif himself may sell for more than LE 60 per square metre, and he gets paid about LE 35 per metre for his work. He can execute very good designs of his own, but also copies those of the Haraneya School, which sell very well. He groups designs into two categories: "faroni" (Pharaonic) or "fellah" (rural) styles.

Although Samira does not weave or dye yarn, she cooks, cleans, and washes for all the workers, besides her own family. She must serve lunch and dinner and feeds additional day workers who may be there. She also runs up and down with tea as they wish. She would like very much to have a house of her own and a safer place for her children, and she pushes Abdel Latif to work very hard to make money for this. If he takes time off she is apt to scold him. As she is from the outskirts of Cairo, her appearance and aims are slightly different from many village women and are compatible with her urban upbringing. She does not wear a *tarha* but ties her hair up in a scarf, and she wears a more urbanised, though still "baladi" style of clothing.

Samira is not looking for work which will pay her a cash income, although she has mentioned that she would like the money. The burdens placed upon her in the household and workshop prevent this. The actual number of her children coincides with the total number of pregnancies. She went to her mother's home in the city for her

76

deliveries, but gave conflicting evidence to the two researchers about who was in attendance. She told one researcher that she was attended by a doctor, but to the other said that a *daya* delivered her. She said she was afraid to deliver in Kerdassa because she has no relatives there. Her husband travelled back and forth to Kerdassa from her mother's during this time. She attended a clinic in Imbaba for her first pregnancy but found this too difficult with the second and third because she had no one to watch the children and had to take them with her. Neighbours in Kerdassa only help her if she is ill. She does not attend the local clinic, preferring to go to a private doctor as she must pay for medicines in either case. Her husband encouraged her to see a doctor during her pregnancies, even though the visits cost LE 1 each.

She has heard of the pill and the loop as contraceptive devices, but in her opinion pills are the safest, cheapest, and most reliable method. Samira worked hard to convince her husband that she should take pills for a short period in order to have time to nurse her baby properly, but she wonders if she is now pregnant again. She feels very tired all the time and does not look well. Nevertheless, she stopped taking the pills under pressure from her husband, who would like to have a son. She would also like a son, but says "I am the one to get tired in the house with the children, not him". When she last talked to us she seemed very dejected.

She heard about family planning from the radio and from relatives and neighbours in the city. She complains that she has trouble finding the kind of pills she is used to and has to change types all the time, which causes her to feel dizzy. She prefers the more expensive pills which are 45 piastres for a month's supply. "The government should help us in using contraceptive methods and not discourage us," she said.

Samira does not think it is important for her daughters to work in the future, but would prefer that they be educated and knowledgeable so that they can make this choice themselves. If they had a university degree, they could decide whether to live in an urban or rural area, and this would improve their ability to make other choices in their lives. No one can predict the future, she feels, and sometime they may need to work. Education, she says, should not differentiate between boys and girls as they both have to struggle to earn a living nowadays. She regrets a great deal that she has not been to school. If she were educated, she says, she would have married a richer man or a man with a fixed income. It annoys her to think that her husband does not have a stable position, but must earn his living "day by day". He forgets about money sometimes, and she has to remind him. She appreciates his other good qualities, like his affectionate attitude towards her and his daughters, and the way he reacts when she encourages him or helps him with his work. "When he sees that I am helping him he is so happy that he never refuses me anything. He buys me clothes and gold."

Samira feels she is different in many ways from the village women and she likes this. She has little contact with neighbours. She enjoys the advantages that her nuclear residence gives her away from her in-laws, yet wishes her mother lived closer, as she has little free time and only manages to see her every few months. She also complains that her husband's constant presence puts strain on her because she feels she has to keep up an appearance of always being active in front of him. Up till now she has felt that the best way to raise the living standards for her family is by helping her husband and by encouraging him to work hard. She does not know what she could do to raise additional cash, and she disdains women who sell in the market. She asked us for advice in this respect.

77

Abdel Latif has had difficulties in the past when he tried to take on outside work to earn more money and recently almost lost his job because of this. As we left he had taken on the responsibility of an additional workshop for his employer and had travelled to recruit new apprentices.

In spite of the conflict between what Samira wants and what she has, this is not reflected in her relationship with her husband, which is still an openly affectionate one. Yet she feels the pressure from this conflict and wishes to improve her life and fulfil her own ambitions more effectively, although she does not know how to do this.

Nasara

Nasara is a small, pretty woman who appears much older than her 23 years. Although she looks very tired, she always greets us with a smile and is ready to chat and prepare tea for us. Her hearty laugh thinly conceals her deeper worries and exhaustion, yet she displays the valued traits of reserve about family problems and does not complain to us. She was chosen as a case study because she is representative of many women in lower income families in Kerdassa who are employed in subsistence crafts. We can also see in her life another example of cross-generational change for traditional craftsmen. Life is difficult for women like Nasara who need money but are unable to seek work outside the home because of social and family obligations and because they lack education and skills.

Nasara's husband Mohamed is a *hoosari*, that is, he manufactures grass mats. He is 30 and they have been married 10 years and have three children, two girls and a boy. Her baby daughter is still being breastfed. This family is locally referred to as a "simple" family, which means that neither set of parents comes from families who own property or who are skilled. They live in the old village in a one-room house with an additional tiny bedroom. The old house was rebuilt with fired brick and cement and has electricity, but water must be carried a considerable distance, mostly up an incline. Nasara makes frequent trips to do this herself as she lacks grown daughters or relatives who can assist her. The house has a clay oven, where she makes all their bread. She has no animals or fowl, except for one duck.

Both Nasara and Mohamed are from the village and neither has attended school. The two elder children go to school or kindergarten and the couple work very hard to give the family a better life. Mohamed's father was a cotton and *versalia* weaver and he learned this craft when he was very young, but, because of low wages and decline in the weaving industry, he went to work for a mat maker when he was 8. Mohamed now runs a small workshop in the main room of his home where he employs three other workers, two adult men and one young boy. He works 10–12 hours daily, seven days a week on the huge floor loom. Three large mats are produced each day which sell for LE 6 each, and special mats may be made to order. Both the red and green dye used for designs and the reeds (*samar*) are obtained from Fayum by a truck, which is rented for LE 40 for the day. About 4,000 *fas* or bunches are bought at a time for LE 400 (10 piastres each). Finished mats are marketed from the house as Mohamed prefers to work on market day.

Nasara is not directly involved in weaving mats, although she assists with preparing the reeds, as does her daughter, 7, and an 8-year old niece who lives next door. She lives around the work of her husband, climbing over the loom which occupies

78

the entire main room of the house. She also has to clean up the dust and debris which is everywhere and prepare tea and food for the workers. She has almost no privacy because of the presence of workers in the house and because the door opens directly onto the narrow and busy street.

Nasara married into her husband's parents' household and continued to care for his mother after his father died. His mother had severe nervous problems and after she died Nasara's own mother came to live with them. She, too, has nervous problems. Because of this and because of the burden placed upon Mohamed by the recent death of his only brother from cancer, the family is considered to be unlucky as well as poor. Responsibility for his brother's wife and five children has fallen on Mohamed, who is respected as a hard worker and a good family man.

Nasara does not seem to be able to take much responsibility and does not participate in any income-producing activities. Her husband's production, however, depends upon her preparation of reeds for the looms, and while the girls are at school she must do this. She tries to see that her daughter and son attend school regularly, which is not easy, as she has no family available to assist her, and her mother is no longer able to help much. *Hasira* mats are used by all local inhabitants, yet there is severe competition between the four local producers and increasingly from imported plastic imitations which are popular because they wear longer and wash more easily, although they are not as comfortable or suited to the environment. The family owns no land and has no access to staple foods which Nasara could use. This strains the budget of the single wage earner.

Because grass mat weaving demands some skill, Mohamed must take a long time to train his apprentices, who are not related to him. He has no unpaid family labour available except in preparing reeds as his son is not yet old enough to work. Women do not weave mats in Egypt. As the prices for mats are highly standardised they do not rise at the same rate as the cost of food and goods which this family must purchase. Although they live without luxuries and have no radio or television, the pressure of life becomes increasingly difficult. The cramped living quarters add to Nasara's problems.

Considering the financial conditions of both families, we have not been able to explain the unusually high brideprice which Mohamed paid to Nasara's family (LE 150).

In all, Nasara has had seven pregnancies, including two spontaneous abortions and two babies who died from diarrhoea after a few days. The *daya* attended her in her own house for five of her deliveries, which were very easy. She registered at the clinic and had a pre-natal check-up. She explained that she must make a quick post-natal recovery in order to look after the other children as there is no one to help her, and also, more importantly, in order to help her husband earn his living. While repeated pregnancies exhaust her and "take away her energy", she feels obliged to continue having children to provide labour to help her husband. After seven pregnancies she feels her health is affected and every effort tires her. The two abortions were very difficult with heavy bleeding which she could not stop, so she went to a hospital in Cairo for treatment.

When she or her children become ill she goes to the public clinic, a private doctor, or to a public hospital in Cairo depending upon the availability of money and the seriousness of the case. The only contraceptive she has heard about is the pill but she has heard it causes bleeding. She used these herself for a short period after her

79

abortions but experienced heavy bleeding at that time, so now leaves everything "in God's hands", saying that "God knows the situation and we have to follow his will in everything". She feels that she does not have enough energy to have any more children and does not want more, but is afraid of using other contraceptive devices about which she knows nothing, as neighbours have told her they affect women's health. Since assuming the added responsibility for his brother's children, her husband does not want more children and has told her to "do something" so that she will not become pregnant. She says she has received no advice concerning family planning methods from the public clinic, where they only sell pills but do not advise on the problem. She hears people discuss family planning when she listens to the radio each morning. She believes she is not able to get pregnant now because she is breastfeeding her baby daughter, but does not know what she will do when she stops.

Nasara wants her children to attend school because she knows that education brings them prestige and increases their probabilities of finding a good job. Sons should be "fully educated" — "I want to see him with the highest certificate possible", she says. As for her daughters, she thinks it is enough for them to complete primary school education (eight years), which is "more than enough" as they "will have to await an early marriage like me". She approves of early marriage for girls because she fears that if they do not they may be thought "wicked, ugly, or incapable of housework ability" and rumours will be spread about them. Yet, she does not want them to be "ignorant".

She thinks that her husband's work is unhealthy and would not like her son to be a *hoosari*. She hastens to add that this was not his original profession or the one he inherited from his father. Besides exhausting him, it does not pay much and she would have "dreamed" of marrying a man with another profession. What can she do now, she asks. She believes her fate is God's will, and she must comply with it.

She complains that the many responsibilities "thrown on her back" exhaust her, that the straw is everywhere and is impossible to remove. Her husband scolds her all the time for her inability to keep the house and the children clean. She does not pay much attention to their appearance, or to her own. We noted that the diet in this household is very poor and think she may also suffer from severe dietary insufficiency, which can only increase if they have to bear all responsibility for five more children. At present, she often cooks for them. She hates helping her husband with his work, as it means she must interrupt her other household chores, although he is always urging her to do so. She envies women who sell goods in the market and who are able to keep the money they earn, as her husband does not pay her for her work. She wishes she could be involved in something that would bring her money, but thinks her husband would beat her if she tried to do so, as he feels it brings shame on him if others see that his wife must work. Then people would think they were poor and he could not support them. Nasara feels she is allowed no decision-making power in the household, but that her husband decides everything. Despite all her problems she tries to accept her *nassib*, or her share in life, but she hopes that the *nassib* of her daughter will be a much better one and that she will marry a "richer" man.

Maryam

Maryam attracted us immediately because of her warmth and the serenity which

80

she exudes. Although one could say she has a marked fatalistic attitude to life, she also seems to have a strong sense of self-esteem and a contentment with life which is reflected in her whole family. She has a very strong productive and marketing role and shares the family business of basket making with her husband, Farag. Both sets of parents came from Kerdassa, and Farag is Maryam's "ibn khalti", her cousin. After 22 years of marriage they have six living children, three boys and three girls. Maryam married at 12 and has had 15 pregnancies, but these statistics have not dimmed the spirit of this small, thin, but still attractive woman of 34.

When not marketing she can always be found at home making baskets, usually on the sunny roof where the family congregates to work. She and Farag and her eldest daughter, 16, are engaged in the manufacture of *sabbat* and *mishana* baskets, popular as shopping baskets in the village and in the city. *Ghab*, a plant like bamboo, is purchased from Sharkeya province for about LE 30–50 per truckload for the *sabbat*, depending upon seasonal fluctuations. Baskets from *ghab* come in two sizes and sell for between 50 piastres and LE 1.50. The *mishana* is a round-bottom basket made from henna sticks. It is widely used locally and prices for these baskets are between 30 and 80 piastres, but Farag is the only one who makes the *mishana* because the sticks are very hard on the hands. Henna sticks also come from Sharkeya and cost LE 15 per load.

Maryam and Farag go to market together, travelling with their donkey cart to the weekly *suq* in their own town and following the market cycle of surrounding towns. Maryam denied that this craft is seasonal but our observations over a year showed that her busy season is during the autumn date harvest when she must go to market six days a week. The rest of the year she travels to market about twice a week. Marketing is a time-consuming task which takes from just after breakfast until three or four in the afternoon, so Sabaah, 16, must take over all household and child-care tasks during this time, and she does this with considerable skill. Maryam does not feel she can take the baby with her to market, as many women do, so she also leaves him in charge of Sabaah, who bottlefeeds him.

This nuclear household is located near the edge of town and the house has recently been rebuilt. Like many village houses, it appears to be in the process of construction, partly due to the high cost of building materials and because it has to adapt to changing family needs. There are three rooms on the ground floor and the oven is on the roof. Electricity and water are brought from across the street. Neither family owns land, and they have no television. Besides the donkey, they raise only chickens.

Maryam never attended school and only two of her six children go. Her eldest son greeted me in English as he returned from primary school. Her daughter who is 8 has had three years of primary schooling.

Despite the fact that they work together, Farag handles all the money, which she thinks is right because, she says, he needs it for their family. She says his job is hard, and admits her own is similarly so. When Maryam's father died "leaving nothing" except his house, Maryam used her share from its sale to help her husband build their new home. She has only one surviving brother and received her inheritance. She is considered an ideal wife in local terms for this act of confidence and generosity as it is known that she did not need to do this, and most women keep their property separate. She is also admired for her obedience to her husband and for her hard work.

Maryam and Farag must work long hours each day to make money to provide basic necessities, and they have almost no surviving family on which to rely in hard times. When she married Farag her brideprice was LE 40. When she was first married she had not begun her periods, but once they started she became pregnant nearly every year. Seven babies died shortly after birth and she has had two spontaneous abortions. She has never considered limiting the size of her family.

All Maryam's children were delivered at home by the local *daya*. Some of those who died were healthy upon arrival but on the seventh day after birth (the *'sebou'*) they died. She did not know why, but the *daya* and some other people told her that this must be the result of the "evil eye". She was unable to breastfeed so chose an expensive brand of powdered milk. We wondered if there was a link between bottlefeeding and the high infant mortality rate in this family. Maryam was convinced after several deaths that it was the result of the "evil eye", so she did not buy new clothes for the arrival of her next babies, but dressed them in very old ones and put a charm (*hegab*) and other objects on them to help ward off the "evil eye". When she did this her babies began to survive.

Both Maryam's parents died when she was young. Her mother died in a public hospital, so that when she was five months pregnant and began to bleed heavily, she was transferred to a public hospital in Cairo for a "D and C" to complete the abortion, as she believed that she, too, was going to die like her mother.

On the whole, her deliveries were very easy. She does not have the money to go to a private doctor and if her children are ill on market days they must wait until she returns before she can take them for care. This is necessary, she says, as the market income is needed each day just for food. "What can you do", she adds. She finds the public clinic "useless", and usually explains the problem to the pharmacist and buys whatever he recommends, without consulting a doctor. She says that "anyway it is done this way in the public clinic as the doctor does not examine the patient".

She feels very tired from so many pregnancies and she knows they drain her health but believes that "it is God who will decide" if she gets pregnant again. Her husband does not think that poverty and a large family are related but believes each child brings its *rizk* (prosperity) and one should not interfere with this. He also thinks that "it is God who must decide". He wants many children as the more he has the more rich and powerful he will feel. While Maryam respects her husband's opinion she prays to God to stop giving her children. She has heard about the pill and the loop but believes that the pill causes bleeding and the loop may cut the womb, so they are both bad. She has learned this from the experience of her neighbours.

Maryam does not want her daughters to go to school, believing both lower and university education are inadvisable for them. She thinks a girl's place is at home and what they learn at school is not helpful to their real lives. Sometimes they learn "poisonous" ideas such as freedom, she says. Then, they think they should not help in the house. Besides, this may be bad for the girl's reputation, as she is seen out of the house all the time and she will be gossiped about and cricitised by the community. This may prevent her from finding a suitable husband. She adds, "What is the importance of education for a girl if anyway she will marry and be obliged to be confined to the house?"

As for boys, she feels they should complete their education, and if God allows, might even enter university and obtain a degree. A boy is different from a girl as he must bring money home to support his family and for this he must find a good job. She wants her boys to be government employees so they would have fixed salaries each month, and because the work is clean and respectable. She does not want them to take over their father's job as a basket maker because it is too tiring and one has to work too hard for a very small return. She would like her daughters to marry government employees, too, and especially hopes they will not marry a peasant (*fellah*) and be in her position, tired all their lives. She wants her daughters to be able to stay at home, just raising children and not forced to help their husbands in their work.

She expects financial assistance from her sons when they are grown and when she becomes older. "Of course it is their duty to assist their mother financially, otherwise why did I worry so much about giving them a good education." She does not expect the same of her daughters as their money will be in the hands of their husbands. Now she has to ask neighbours to help her if she needs money.

Maryam likes her husband and tries to treat him, as he treats her, with respect. He says she has "a heart of gold" and, because she is an orphan and has no one but him, he must be nice to her. She feels it is her duty to help him in his work, and this way she saves the expense of workers whom they would have to employ to do this work. She says she only works because she has to, and if she paid workers the family would have even less to live on. Carrying baskets to nearby villages along the dusty and difficult roads is not easy and exhausts her. Although she considers Farag a good family head, caring for his house and children foremost and not spending his leisure outside the house, she wishes she had not married a basket maker. She sees life as a continuous struggle. She tries to be an understanding wife, hardly asking him for anything, even when she wants a new dress or clothes for the children. Her aims are modest, simply to raise her children and to feed them properly. Sometimes she is glad that they do not have many relatives, as this makes her closer to Farag "and their hearts compassionate upon each other".

Maryam acknowledges the heavy household and child-care role Sabaah carries and knows that if it were not for her, she could not work so often, because the other children are very young. She worries about what she would do if Sabaah should marry and leave her. "Her other sisters will have to take over", Maryam says with her usual resigned smile.

We see no conflict in Maryam's life despite all its difficulties. Her deep religious faith has assisted her to overcome all her worries and troubles, and she modestly finds pleasure in "accepting God's plans".

Nafisa

Nafisa is the daughter of one of the five brothers responsible for so many changes in the weaving industry in Kerdassa and who were the main organisers of weaving during the present century. Her father is very old now, around 85, and is no longer active in the trade to Sudan, Chad, and the Libyan Arab Jamahiriya, although he still maintains an office in the centre of the old bazaar in Cairo. Her father had three wives, and Nafisa is a daughter of his second wife, who has been separated from him for a considerable time. Her mother lives in the village with one married son.

The status of the family as a whole is very high, both because of their important role as merchants and weavers in the past and because her cousin operates the largest and most lucrative tourist trade in textiles in the village. A number of her father's children have gone to work for this cousin, while others have dispersed into other occupations. Nafisa's marriage to a basket maker must have been difficult for her, as merchants generally disdain manual labour here. She is now 39 and has been married to her husband for 28 years. She has almost no contact with most of the members of her father's family and has no claim for assistance on him. Her marriage choice may have been limited by the separation or divorce, but at any rate, her husband is considered greatly beneath the status of her father's family.

Nafisa lives in an extended family with her husband and five children, 17 years to 5 months. Her eldest daughter, 17, has returned to her father's house with her one-year old son after her divorce. Daughters are not always welcomed back when they have trouble with their husbands, especially on a permanent basis. Nafisa expresses disappointment that her daughter married young rather than finishing school. A 14-year-old son and 9-year-old daughter are now at school. Neither parent has been to school.

The family lives in a modest home amongst a cluster of *khoos* workers and merchants. There is both electricity and running water in the house, along with a television and an oven. Nafisa cares for the donkey they use in their marketing and raises chickens in the house. Farag's father owned a reasonable amount of land, but because he had so many brothers it was subdivided into small portions and he has only 11 *kirat* now. He lets this land out "b'nuss" (by half), the most common customary arrangement for sharecropping, although in this case he supplies fertiliser and so collects more than half of the crop or sale price. As joint reckonings are no longer the custom, he has trouble knowing precisely what the crop yields are.

Farag comes from three generations of *maktaf* craftsmen (*khawass*). He specialises in only two of the many local products made from palm leaf, a two-handled carrying basket and a donkey-carrying basket which comes in pairs. He works at home, employing one young man. Nafisa performs three of the four processes in basket making, but is considered only a "helper", although his production depends upon the rate of her work. Although the only process which she does not do is sewing up the braided strips, she is not considered by the community to be a craftsman, as is her husband. Even where heads of households are women who may have taken over a family craft business they are not referred to by an occupational title but may be said to be assisting a son, brother, etc.

Twice a week Farag markets his products, taking his donkey cart to the village market or to those in surrounding villages. He must compete with the merchants in his village, some of whom have extensive cottage industries in *khoos* products. Nafisa has denied that she accompanies him to market, but we have seen her there. However, she does not travel to the surrounding villages with him.

The brideprice paid by Farag for Nafisa was LE 70, which may be compared with that of her daughter, which was LE 700. Nafisa was married at the age of 11 and has had 12 pregnancies. Seven babies died shortly after birth and she has had no spontaneous abortions. Besides her mother and neighbours, a *daya* always attended her deliveries, which were very difficult. When her daughter gave birth, the *daya* also attended, but because complications arose a doctor was summoned and she was eventually moved to a hospital for delivery.

Nafisa does not like going to the public clinic as she feels they give no care to patients and do not give medication. During her first two pregnancies she was registered at the public clinic but decided it was useless, and stopped attending after that. She thinks she has enough children. At the moment she is breastfeeding her baby and in the past she has always become pregnant once she stops breastfeeding, so this time she intends to have a loop inserted. She has discussed this with her husband and he agreed as he can see her health is poor. She thinks that pills affect the health and therefore the loop is better. Like "everyone", she says, she has heard of family planning from the radio.

Nafisa is very explicit about her regret that she did not give her eldest daughter an education and that she "married her" very young. She says with sorrow, "Look, here is the result. She has had very bad luck and if she didn't have her father's home to return to what would her future be without any education or work?" The constant reminder of this "bad example" reinforces Nafisa's goal to educate both her remaining sons and her daughters. She wants to give them education which will be useful and directs a lot of her energy to this. "This is enough", she says, "let us not repeat the tragedy." Besides the radical change in Nafisa's attitudes toward education, she now thinks it might be useful for girls to work so they would not be dependent on others for financial support.

Nafisa wants her children to realise things which were impossible for her. Although she thinks her husband a good-hearted fellow who cares for her and provides for her needs, she would have preferred to marry a government employee so she would not have had to work so hard for so little reward. She wants her daughters to marry government workers and believes their lives would then be better than hers. At the same time, she realises that her position as the daughter of a respected merchant has given her certain privileges that other women do not have. As one would expect in this instance, her husband trusts her and gives her responsibilities. He sees she is honest and manages the household well, and does not let his children want for anything, therefore he lets her decide how to spend the household budget.

She says she is not really able to think whether her life with her husband has been "fulfilling" or not. It is too late to think this way as she is old, and she feels that her *nassib* (fate) has been fulfilled. She would have preferred not to marry so young as she would first have understood life better and perhaps then have had the courage to refuse. She thinks this even though he is "worth marrying" and treats her very well.

Nafisa gets the greatest pleasure in raising and caring for children. She would have liked very much to have been allowed to stay at home just to do this and not to be forced to have the responsibility of helping her husband in his work, as she must do now. She knows that this is her duty and she tries to do it well. She is grateful that she does not have to prepare meals or tea for workers. When they do have workers they "must manage on their own". Nafisa's divorced daughter does most of the work inside the household, such as cooking and cleaning, and helping to care for the younger children.

Nafisa's acceptance of a life which is not one which she would have chosen and which, given her family standing, she finds beneath expectations gives her a modicum of peace and minimises any conflict which might otherwise be present.

Hamida

The household of the traditional blacksmith (*hadad*) is an interesting one, both because it is polygamous, and because it is part of an endogamous clan. The living conditions of this family are the most difficult we encountered and the productive role of women the heaviest. The house, which is an ancient structure very little of which is left standing, lies at the outskirts of the village next to the date palm grove. The family lives mostly outdoors, little protected from either sun or cold. These "traditional" blacksmiths are somewhat separated from the community and intermarry with other blacksmith families, who are related and who live either locally or in adjoining villages. Apprentices are also sought from the family rather than from outside, thus endogamy is occupation-related. The community acknowledges the important service the blacksmith provides to farmers and householders, making and repairing essential tools and furnishings.

Hamida is 40, she has been married to Orini, 45, for 10 years, and is the mother of one 3-year-old son. She is his second wife, her co-wife having borne four children. Besides the two wives and their children, the joint household contains the orphaned son of an uncle, 12. One married daughter has moved away. There is electricity in the house but no water and no oven. Water must be brought from relatives across the street, and they use the oven belonging to other neighbours. The women keep several animals, at present four goats, two sheep, and two calves. Hamida married into this household from a village some distance away, where she claims to be a daughter of Orini's grandfather.

Hamida's productive role is unusual in Egypt, where men do so many tasks reserved for females in other countries (e.g. spinning). In most countries, smithing is rarely part of women's work. Both of Orini's wives actually swing hammers along with men in order to pound hot iron into shape. Women also operate the bellows, while other males carry out the more skilled tasks and maintain the fire. Orini is presently training his nephew and an elder son to do this. Because it takes a long time to train a blacksmith and because they do not wish to share their "secrets" with non-relatives, apprentices are not taken from outside the family. The occupational title here refers to the family as a group, including its female members. All are called *hadad* or *hadadeen* (pl).

Actual firing and production is done for three or four hours a day. Coal is purchased from a market on the edge of the city and transported by rented truck or bicycle. If they run out, they cannot work until someone fetches more coal, and they sometimes have to work in the evenings to make up for this. Some products are manufactured from scrap which customers bring and some are made from the scrap in the workshop. Although the co-wives claim to share all tasks, we note that Hamida goes to market goods while her co-wife is more involved in cooking, laundry and domestic tasks. Before her recent operation Hamida used to sell in the village streets, walking about to hawk wares and travelling to surrounding villages, but she is now limited to selling in the weekly *suq*.

No one in the family has attended school and this is considered customary, although an uncle's son is at school and they are very proud that he is the best student in his class. Informants tell us that in spite of the difficult nature of the work it is not difficult for these smiths to obtain wives, as the work is considered essential to the village. We have no information on how many wives come from outside the family.

The brideprice paid for Hamida was LE 30, and Orini had paid LE 10 for his first wife. It is reasonable to believe that she was taken as a second wife for her working potential. Both wives look older than their years, tired, and dirty. Hamida had two sets of twins, but both deliveries were difficult and all the babies died. She sought medical advice for the first time after she lost her second twins and a goitre operation was recommended. After this was performed, her present, healthy son was born. Her deliveries except the last, which was in a public hospital in Giza, were all at home, attended by a *daya*. The heavy work may lead to lowered fertility in this case or to spontaneous abortion. Inadequate diet may also lower fertility. Sanitary standards are very low in what remains of the household structure.

Neither woman has registered at the public clinic and all the co-wives' children were delivered by the *daya*. When children are ill, they are taken to the clinic, since the co-wives cannot afford a private doctor or even a public hospital where they are obliged to tip, and they do not like the clinic very much. Hamida wants more children and hopes she will get pregnant as soon as she stops breastfeeding her son. Her husband would also like her to bear more children. She has heard about the pill and the loop but thinks that they are very bad for the health. She thinks the doctors in the public clinic neglect poor patients, and for her the *daya* is "better than one hundred doctors".

Hamida wants her son to be educated "until the end", that is, to university degree standard. She tries to save some of the money her husband gives her for this because she feels it is not so important to her husband and when the time comes he may not find the money for school fees. He may prefer his son to help him in his work. She sees education as the way to save him from being a blacksmith and she exerts every effort in this direction. She expects him to help her in the future as this is his duty, and "why else would a mother get so tired raising him?"

Hamida complains constantly about her work in smithing, which she feels is exhausting and difficult and is not financially rewarding. If she had had a choice, she would have preferred not to marry a blacksmith, but "everything in life cannot be adapted to one's own will, this is a *nassib* (fate) and one has to adapt to it and accept it". She believes that if one hates what one does, one will become ill; therefore she has made a great effort to like her work, and thinks she has succeeded. Now it is easier for her to work near a very hot fire and to manipulate the iron. She says the work is not limited by hours, and she must work very long days. She also gets satisfaction from the admiration and appreciation of her husband, which, for her, is a great recompense. Her husband does not earn much and relies on her because otherwise he would have to employ another worker. She finds that the more she works and helps him, the more she gains his love. She knows that her husband married her so that she could help him in his work, and that he wanted one wife to bear children and take care of the house and one wife to help him. When we talked to him, he said that he thinks it is preferable for a woman to help her husband rather than seek outside work, and that he likes very much having Hamida to help him. Hamida admitted later that she does not take responsibility for household tasks and that this is the sole responsibility of her co-wife who bakes bread, cooks, washes, and looks after the children and animals. Hamida does not even do the daily shopping for the family.

Hamida wishes she could earn a lot of money, which she would then use to take a rest from her very difficult work of smithing. This is her main aim in life.

Bibliography

Anker, R. 1980 and 1981. *Research on women's roles and demographic change: Survey questionnaires for households, women, men and communities with background explanations.* Geneva, ILO.

Anker, R., Buvinic, M. and Youssef, N. (eds.) 1982. *Women's roles and population trends in the Third World.* London, Croom Helm.

Baer, G. 1964. *Egyptian guilds in modern times.* Jerusalem, Israel Oriental Society.

Beck, L. and Keddie, N. (eds.) 1978. *Women in the muslim world.* Cambridge, Harvard University Press.

Boserup, E. 1970. *Women's role in economic development.* New York, St. Martins Press.

Buvinic, M. 1976. *Women and world development: An annotated bibliography.* Overseas Development Council, Washington.

CAPMAS 1976. *Population Census.* Cairo, CAPMAS.

Church, K. 1981. *Focussed biographies, draft coding manual activities and expectations.* Geneva, ILO; mimeographed.

Connell, J. and Lipton, M. 1977. *Assessing village labour situations in developing countries.* Delhi, Oxford University Press.

Friedman, H. 1980. "Household production and the national economy: Concepts for the analysis of agrarian formations", in *Journal of Peasant Studies* (London), Vol. 7, No. 2, pp. 158–184.

Gadalla, S. 1978. *Is there hope?* Cairo, The American University in Cairo Press.

Goldschmidt-Clermont, L. 1982. *Unpaid work in the household: A review of economic evaluation methods*, Women, Work and Development Series, No. 1. Geneva, ILO.

Goody, J. 1973. "Bridewealth and dowry in Africa and Eurasia", in Goody, Jack and Tambiah, S.D. *Bridewealth and dowry.* Cambridge, Cambridge University Press.

Gran, J. 1977. "Impact of the world market on Egyptian women", in *Merip Reports* (Washington) No. 58.

Harik, I. 1979. *Distribution of land, employment and income in rural Egypt.* New York, Cornell Rural Development Committee.

Ibrahim, Magdi Abd el Kader 1980. "Demographic aspects of rural new settlement with special reference to fertility and mortality patterns: A case study in IBIS extension area, Egypt", M. Phil. thesis. UN–ARE Cairo Demographic Center.

Long, N. and Richardson, P. 1978. "Informal sector, petty commodity production and the social relations of small-scale enterprise", in Clammer, John (ed.): *The new economic anthropology*. London, Maxmillan Press.

Loza, S. 1981. *Egypt I and II*. Liège, International Union for the Scientific Study of Population.

Mabro, R. and Radwan, S. 1976. *The industrialization of Egypt, 1939–1973*. Oxford, Clarendon Press.

Morsy, S.A. 1978. "Sex differences and folk illness in an Egyptian village", in Beck, L. and Keddie, N. (eds.): *Women in the Muslim world*. Cambridge, Harvard University Press.

Mueller, E. 1982. "The allocation of women's time and its relation to fertility", in Anker, R., Buvinic, M. and Youssef, N.H.: *Women's roles and population trends in the Third World*. London, Croom Helm.

Nagi, M.H. 1971. *Labor force and employment in Egypt, A demographic and socioeconomic analysis*. Indiana, Praeger Publishing.

Nour, el Sayed 1979. "Mortality level, patterns and differentials in Egypt". UN Economic Commission for Africa.

Oppong, C. 1980. *A synopsis of seven roles and status of women: An outline of a conceptual and methodological approach,* Population and Labour Policies Programme working paper. Geneva, ILO; mimeographed.

Oppong, C. and Church, K. 1981. *A field guide to research on seven roles of women, focussed biographies*, Population and Labour Policies Programme working paper. Geneva, ILO; mimeographed.

Peters, E.L. 1978. "The status of women in four Middle East communities", in Beck, L. and Keddie, N. (eds.): *Women in the Muslim world*. Cambridge, Harvard University.

Shanin, T. 1972. *The awkward class*. Oxford, Clarendon Press.

Staffa, S.J. 1977. *Conquest and fusion. The social evolution of Cairo A.D. 642–1850*. Leiden, Brill.

Tucker, J. 1976. "Egyptian women in the work force: An historical survey", in *Merip Reports* (Washington), No. 50.

White, E.H. 1978. "Legal reform as an indicator of women's status in Muslim nations", in Beck, L. and Keddie, N. (eds.): *Women in the Muslim world*. Cambridge, Harvard University Press.

Youssef, N.H. 1974. *Women and work in developing societies*, Population Monograph Series No. 15. Berkeley, University of California.